Steinerbooks *The S* ... format, 4-3/ ...

Meditations on Signs of Zodiac, *Jocelyn* / 1701 / $1.95
The Count of Saint-Germain, *Cooper-Oakley* / 1702 / $1.95
The Unknown Philosopher: Saint-Martin, *Waite* / 1703 / $2.45
Alchemists Through the Ages, *Waite* / 1704 / $1.95
From Sphinx To Christ: An Occult History, *Schuré* / 1705 / $1.95
Reincarnation and Immortality, *Steiner* / 1706 / $1.95
Education As An Art, *Steiner* / 1707 / $1.95
Ancient Mysteries of East: Rama / Krishna, *Schuré* / 1708 / $1.45
Mysteries of Ancient Egypt: Hermes / Moses, *Schuré* / 1709 / $1.45
Mysteries of Ancient Greece: Orpheus / Plato, *Schuré* / 1710 / $1.45
Ancient Mysteries of Delphi: Pythagoras, *Schuré* / 1711 / $1.45
The Light of the Mysteries: Jesus, *Schuré* / 1712 / $1.45
Methods of Spiritual Research, *Steiner* / 1713 / $1.45
Results of Spiritual Investigation, *Steiner* / 1714 / $1.45
Gardening For Health: The Organic Way, *Philbrick* / 1715 / $1.45
Cosmic Memory: Atlantis and Lemuria, *Steiner* / 1716 / $1.95
Atlantis / Europe: Secret of the West, *Merejkowski* / 1717 / $2.45
Ragnarök: Destruction of Atlantis, *Donnelly* / 1718 / $2.45
Occult Mysteries of Christianity, *Steiner* / 1719 / $1.95
Lamps of Western Mysticism, *Waite* / 1720 / $1.95
Eleven European Mystics, *Steiner* / 1721 / $1.95
Caspar Hauser: Enigma of a Century, *Wasserman* / 1722 / $2.45
Zanoni: A Rosicrucian Tale, *Bulwer-Lytton* / 1723 / $2.45
Atlantis: The Antediluvian World, *Donnelly* / 1724 / $2.45
Vril: The Power of the Coming Race, *Bulwer-Lytton* / 1725 / $1.95
The Golem: Mystical Tales from the Prague Ghetto, *Bloch* / 1726 / $1.95
Mysteries of Egypt: The Secret Rites of the Nile, *Spence* / 1727 / $1.95
The Pictorial Key to the Tarot, *Waite* / 1728 / $1.95
Queen Móo and the Egyptian Sphinx, *LePlongen* / 1729 / $2.45
ESPecially IRENE: A Guide to Psychic Awareness, *Hughes* / 1730 / $1.65

Additional titles in preparation. Send for complete catalog.
Rudolf Steiner Publications, Blauvelt, N.Y. 10913, U.S.A.

ESPecially Irene
A Guide to Psychic Awareness

by
Irene F. Hughes

Rudolf Steiner Publications
Blauvelt, New York 10913, U.S.A.

Library of Congress Catalogue Card Number:
70–189997

First printing

Printed in the United States of America

Contents

Foreword

Whether we are "believers" in psychic phenomena or view it with "open-minded" skepticism or even total disbelief, there isn't one of us who at some time or other hasn't secretly yearned for a glimpse into the future.

Though few are gifted with extra-sensory perception, or clairvoyance, to the degree attained by Irene Hughes, we can acquire these powers to a lesser degree.

And that's what this book is all about.

Not only does Mrs. Hughes reveal in these pages how one can acquire inner knowledge of one's future but what is more important, she opens the door to a new life style—"spiritual awareness"—leading to inner peace and happiness. A dream, a vision, a goal to be lived.

A clairvoyant since early childhood, Irene Hughes is an acknowledged authority on ESP and all related phases including clairvoyance, clairaudience, telepathy, psychometry, precognition and retrocognition.

For many years she has been engaged in psychical research and serious study of paranormal phenomena not only to make the best use of her God-given talent to benefit mankind, but also to teach others how to develop their latent psychic abilities.

In this book, written with great clarity and easy-to-understand language, Irene Hughes shares her experiences and expert knowledge of how to tap the all-important "sixth" sense leading to "spiritual awareness" that will help bring peace and a better life to an intolerant and strife-torn world.

Mrs. Hughes has earned for herself worldwide recognition as an outstanding psychic sensitive through her phenomenal ability to accurately foretell future events. Through her column, "ESPecially Irene," that has appeared weekly for the past six years in the Chicago-based Community Publications newspaper chain, she is known to hundreds of thousands of readers who subscribe to the publication on a local, national and world-wide basis.

Mrs. Hughes has had her own television program, has appeared for many years on television and radio here and abroad and has lectured before many hundreds of groups throughout the world.

As a member of the editorial staff of Community Publications newspapers, I have been privileged to have been closely associated with Irene Hughes, professionally and as a friend. But apart from my regard for her, a dear friend, I have the sincerest admiration for her genuine ability as a psychic, for her integrity and the use she has made of her special gift to benefit mankind.

For the seriously interested, for those who would gain knowledge and insight into a new dimension of the mind, I highly commend this book by Irene F. Hughes.

Patricia Bartelt
December 23, 1971

1

My Psychic Tie-up with Apollo 13! The "Scorpion"! 3 Astronauts Die!

Restless sleep, punctuated by sounds of sonic space-ship problems, ended abruptly. I sat up in bed, shaking my head to get the sounds of astronauts' voices away from me. I thought the radio on the bookcase bed had been turned on and the play-by-play account of a space journey by some of our astronauts was tuned in. Wide awake now, I looked around me. No radio on—no one stirring, even though it was 7:00 A.M.

Suddenly, I realized that I was experiencing a psychic situation concerning the oncoming

Apollo 13 flight. I *knew* that the men were becoming ill! I *knew* that there would be a liquid-oxygen explosion in the air and possibly a fire on the ground. I *knew* that the three astronauts would never reach the moon, but would have to return—distressed and disappointed, with one of them having a fever and ill.

My feet touched the floor lightly as I rushed out of the bedroom to wash my face and brush my teeth, hoping that the feelings beyond reality would go away. But they did not. I realized at that time that I was experiencing clairvoyance—and definitely felt that I was right with the astronauts and living the entire trip. Perhaps my astral body had also played a part in arriving at the scene where plans were under way—but it was still three days before the flight!

I picked up the telephone and dialed the number of Colonel M. in the Washington, D.C., area. It was now 8:00 A.M. Chicago time—9:00 A.M. there. My impulse was to tell him, since he had been associated with NASA in the past and was still in government service in the Washington area. No one answered. Frantically, but yet calmly, I dialed the number of another colonel who lived nearby Colonel M. His wife answered, and since we were long-time friends, I lost no time in giving her all of my impressions and urging her to contact Colonel M. later that morning and be certain that he followed through on giving the information to NASA.

That night I called back and talked to Colonel M. I repeated all the problems that I saw in connection with the Apollo 13 flight, and he assured me that he had given these impressions to NASA. "Of course, Irene, you know that we can never say that they followed through on them—but I gave them to the Chief over there." "Colonel, the Astronauts are becoming ill—they must be checked out. And that liquid-oxygen explosion will occur in space—they'll never set down on the moon this time, but will return safely, although one of them will have fever and be ill."

In his usual calm voice, Colonel M. said: "What will cause the explosion—some tampering beforehand?" "No," I said, "I see an electric wire that's hanging loose and it looks like it is very near a fan." "What kind of a fan?" asked the Colonel. "A fan just like the round ones you plug in and use in the summertime," I said. "Where is it located on the ship—is it inside the main cabin, or just where?" he asked. "It's in what looks like a second section—a small room outside of the main one, it seems to me." "All right, I'll get the information to NASA."

After the Apollo 13 took off, everyone knew of the problems. I went to the theater with my husband and a couple from Hawaii. During the intermission, I left and called the Colonel again. "I'm so concerned about the flight—watch it closely as there will be that liquid-oxygen explosion." "Why do you say liquid oxygen," he asked. "Because I see clear liquid spilling over the outside of the space ship and I see flames rushing over it, but the explosion will happen inside of the ship." "I'll speak to NASA again—and we'll watch closely," he promised.

Then came the explosion and the worry and concern for the safety of the astronauts. I called yet again and said, "Don't worry, the men *will* get back safe and sound, but one of them will be ill." "Doesn't look good for them," said the colonel. "We're really concerned that they won't make it at all—if only they can by-pass the moon and head for home." "They will," I reassured him. "For seven years, I've given you impressions of various national affairs and international ones, as well as personal ones—and they've been accurate, even to the deaths of the three astronauts the time the space ship burned. Remember, Colonel, I told you about that and you taped it." "Yes, I remember—only I forgot about the tape until it was too late."

I bade him good-by and hung up. Hours of watching and waiting—and then my good friend, Mercedes McCambridge, came into town for TV appearances and to take the female lead in a play. We were having lunch at the Pump Room—she had invited me to come along since she was going to participate in the Fashion Show and talk about her appearance. The hostess also asked me to give my impressions of Apollo 13, which I did. The ship had not yet landed, so no one could deny my predictions: sad to say, they came to pass. How much better if they had been fully heeded, with an additional check on the wiring system where liquid oxygen was stored or being used! What a fantastic amount of money could have been saved, as well as materials—and a lot of wear and tear on the physical condition of the astronauts! Just because this was, to some, an unorthodox method of "knowing" things, the great scientists associated with the space program couldn't begin to acknowledge—at least not openly—the voice of a modern-day prophet.

After my predictions of the three astronauts' deaths by fire in the space ship; after my prediction, in 1966, of an oncoming fantastic and unbelievable snowstorm that would hit Chicago on January 26, 27, 28, and 29 and again on February 1–4 in 1967, it would seem that those in high positions might pay a bit of attention—if for no other reason than to scoff should these things not come to pass. How could they possibly heed my pleas, when I was a lone voice—lost in the masses. Why should I know those things when they couldn't know with all of their technological knowledge? Could I prevent the images and vibrations from surrounding me and forcing me to make the predictions known? I wouldn't dare to prevent them—since mankind has, since the beginning of life, relied upon his intuition and inner knowing more than anything else.

About the prediction of the impending deaths of the three astronauts by fire: I was visiting in Washington, D.C., as I did several times each year. Colonel M., Colonel G., Lieutenant Commander S., their families, and the daughter of General Patton, all gathered one evening for good comradeship and some predictions. Earlier that evening, I had talked to Colonel M. and his lovely wife, M., and it was at that time that he taped the prediction that "there would be a fire in the wiring system of the second section of the space ship and three Astronauts would be burned to death." Colonel M. had asked me to describe what I could about it, and I said I saw a space ship that seemed to be two—a second section—in which the wiring was faulty. I saw numerous wiring, in and out, and overlapping, and this seemed to be in a recessed area completely around the second section of the ship. I saw smoke and flashes of fire and heard the screams of one of the astronauts as the three of them burned to death.

The colonel asked several other questions, and then we closed the session. Later, when the fire occurred, I told the colonel that I felt it was Chaffee's screams that I had clairvoyantly heard. Something that I did not tell him but which I definitely felt was that a very emotionally unstable person had worked on the wiring system and had really fouled it up! The colonel remarked to me, after it had happened —the taping had taken place quite a long time before—that he wept when he remembered the tape. Why *didn't* he remember it? That's one of the mysteries of life which I feel falls into the category of one's "destiny beyond change." No one was to change it, just as no one was to change the deaths of Jack and Robert Kennedy—or the death of Martin Luther King. When the finger of Fate writes the date of transformation, the flash of change will come about in time and the deed will be done, even though man may try to interfere or prevent it.

Later on, at another session taped by the colonel, I mentioned that an atomic submarine would be lost, and I gave the approximate date. I said "there will actually be two," and I gave the San Francisco area as one of the places. The colonel said he took the tape to the naval officer in command, but that he scoffed at the idea, saying, "No atomic submarine has been lost to date, and I don't believe it." Too bad that because of the personal and different philosophical persuasions of that man, we lost a valuable and expensive submarine. Why couldn't he say, "Well, this may be coming from what I call a crackpot, but I'll try to check it out anyway—won't do any harm"?

My prediction included these points: There

would be an oil leak, and the submarine would explode and all would be lost. I felt that it would go down very near the area of another ship. I indicated that I felt that particular submarine had been "tracked" for at least three or four days by a Russian submarine, but that the loss would be from within and not because of an attack. I felt that I could see a most unusual panel—like a secret compartment—on the submarine, and I felt that someone had tried to push some of those buttons and that they had jammed. Also, I could feel the pressure building up within that submarine, see the oil spilling out over the top, and see a huge crack and the boat's beginning descent into the water. One of the most unusual impressions came when suddenly, I could hear, very loud and clear, the sonic tones given off by the submarine, and I felt "tied psychically" to it until its death. That was a terribly frightening experience, because I could not free myself from that situation; I tried to turn my thoughts from it, but it was no use. I wept, and asked within me for someone to hear and do something about it. When I was asked to determine on a map where it went down, I first told a friend, a local judge, that it was four hundred miles away from Hawaii. But I changed my mind and let names which were only partially correct creep in. My original and first impression was absolutely correct.

Another interesting incident connected with

this was a call to me from Wally Phillips of WGN Radio in Chicago. I was in Springfield to appear on a radio show, and a lady called Wally and told him that I had predicted that a submarine would go down. Someone connected with her family—or a local-area resident—was involved and she wanted to call the Naval Station in Virginia and have them call me, and wanted Wally to get my permission to accept the call. I agreed, and so a naval officer from Virginia called me in Springfield. I gave him my impressions—very reluctantly. I felt I was talking to a cold, stone wall.

However, he called back and asked for further impressions, and I gave them to him. I then wrote out my report and gave it to another friend in the navy. In that report, I changed my original impression—and to this day, I'll regret it. You can believe that now I stick to the original impressions—and they usually turn out to be correct. That was another incident that I felt could perhaps have been partially prevented—by someone checking out the workings of the submarine before it left. I feel that no matter how I, as a clairvoyant, "see psychically," or "sense beyond the five acknowleged senses" a situation of national import—it should be listened to and checked out. I feel that our nation could benefit in countless situations—if those in high positions would take a moment to listen—if these things were checked out; then the decision could be made as to whether the check was worth while. In all the cases mentioned thus far, only a few man hours and a little money would have resulted in lives and valuable equipment saved.

You *do* remember the submarine that sank in San Francisco, don't you? Why didn't those in authority—after the "Scorpion" was lost—listen to the predictions about *that* submarine? Could it be that there are "Communist-controlled minds" in our midst that say, "there's no such thing as ESP, thought-reading, etc."? The years ahead will tell—beyond any doubt. And those who stop in any way our nation and those at its helm from preventing the inner destruction of this nation, or the destruction—deliberately or otherwise—of our space ships and naval fleets, our planes and the lives of our men—are they not just as guilty of treason or of murder as though they had dealt the death blow themselves? Perhaps their pride would have been wounded by the "inner knowing" of a nontechnical person. Perhaps they *did* spend years becoming psychologists or specialized scientists—so what? If someone has wisdom beyond the knowledge that some person in the long ago wrote down as the *only* way things can be done—should we not try the different ways?

This age of "seeing through" everything under the sun and near it will bring about, I predict, a total revolution in man's thought and actions and beliefs about what we now call the field of extrasensory perception. I predict that, for the next hundred years, the mystical arts will be the way through which man finally realizes that, in seeing signs and wonders, he can turn to a force of great energy—perhaps greater than any atomic energy—and in recognizing it as his god, use it in every area of life: for greater understanding between nations; for unbelievably quick methods for healing numerous and diverse diseases; and for revelations of the workings of man's brain and that elusive energy, man's mind!

If there is evidence of men who lived four- and five-billion years ago, and rocks and other things seem to point to it, then why would it not be feasible that those men had reached the pinnacle of wisdom and in so doing came to total destruction? Perhaps man since then is merely picking up—slowly—the energy in the universe and materializing it into knowledge of scientific endeavors that will, in turn, destroy *us* totally, unless we reach a new pinnacle of spiritual wisdom. We must use these vast energies of wisdom to create a new universe, and many worlds within this universe, where man can live in outer space, beneath the waters of the lakes and oceans, and in near space—all because he took time, voluntarily and unrestrictedly, to learn to live in "inner space."

2

How I, Personally, Feel That ESP Works in My Life

First of all, we need some definitions of what extrasensory perception is. I believe that the very word "extrasensory" frightens people and causes them to feel that it is something weird, way-out, unorthodox, or supernatural. That is not so. The extrasensory abilities involve feeling, seeing, sensing, touching, and tasting—without the use of the five acknowledged senses. Modern man feels that he has all of the answers in theology or in some ideology and does not wish to go too far beyond what he can see with his physical eyes or hear with his physical ears. How restricted he is!

All things in life have symbols and when I, as a psychic, see a symbol it then turns into a sound which I say is a voice within me. Now this is natural, because, after all, man can only understand communication by means of the five senses; no matter what happens in an unusual way, it really must be transmitted to man in a way that requires the use of his senses. When I say I hear a voice within me, I lean forward to try to catch it with my physical ear, even though I *know* that the sound is within me. Perhaps I have seen a symbol, an image if you will, of a bell, and knowing that that bell will ring, lean forward to hear it. But does that bell mean someone by the name of Bell, or does it signify a particular church? To me, extrasensory perception is an adventure in spirit, and a very beautiful adventure at that. There are many ways in which one can develop his individual psychic abilities but one must first of all be aware of the ability he wishes to develop. Do you have ESP? Of course you do, because all men were born with these inherent abilities. Let us consider clairvoyance, which means, simply, "clear seeing"; but that is not enough for me. My own definition of it is that it is the expansion of the third eye, or of sight that is gained through energies that flow toward the aura of my body or that flow within the solar plexus. The moment these energies, coming perhaps from a great distance, such as another country touch me, then I can immediately see what is happening in that area. On the other hand, I may not have any physical reaction at all as I sit quietly and just watch the scene before me in Africa or Japan or China, or wherever my thoughts may be directed at that particular moment.

I do not wish to use elaborate words in these pages but to give simple explanations because I would like this book to be a teaching manual. Therefore, I will explain as simply as possible.

I must indicate here that there is a method of preparation for the use of these spiritual abilities which is extremely important and should be considered first of all. The body must be totally clean, and the mind peaceful and clear of any fault-finding or unenlightened thoughts. The person must sit in a very relaxed way or lie down and center the eyes upward on the third eye. As this is done, a feeling as of watching waves coming in from the ocean should flow through the mind and help to relax the entire body; as the waves wash in and out, the individual sends forth all of the problems from his body and mind and brings in strength and harmony and peace. After about fifteen minutes, the person is ready to concentrate upon the third eye more intensely and from that point on, he can just relax and watch for any symbols that may appear. If he is gifted with clairvoyance, then certainly some image will begin to appear. It may be insignificant or vague, but it will appear. At the very moment that the first images appear, the individual begins the slow shedding of old things and old ways and old ideas of the earth. From that time forth, the person can progress spiritually and begin to expand in other areas of psychic development. One of these areas is that of clairsentience, or the sensing of things that are to be. It may manifest itself as an uneasy emotion, as anxiety, or as happiness, but it is clairsentience. These emotions come without any object visibly creating them. When we learn to control these extrasensory emotions then we can begin to be aware of the ideas associated with them.

Another area of ability is psychometry. I feel that when I touch an object belonging to someone else that it instantly tells me whether or not that person is a calm, cool person, whether he is emotionally upset, or whether he is just nervous because of a particular situation. I feel that in most cases of psychometry the names of people involved in past experiences—such as someone who has died a violent death—may come through first just by my touching the object. Names have a sound to them, but I must be able to hear them because that's the way that I've been taught; there is no erratic or unusual method used at all in the field of ESP.

That conception is in the minds of some psychologists and psychiatrists who feel that it is not a true way of understanding life.

When I am very quiet in prayer and meditation I often hear an earthquake; with the first sounds come the images of it and its possible location. When I first hear them the sounds are outside of me and I am alerted to them through my body, not necessarily through my ears; but since hearing with the ears is natural, I strain forward to try to hear more clearly, at the same time recognizing that this won't work. What I must then do is to relax even more, to sit very quietly, and not be disturbed by any situation at hand, in order that I may hear more clearly the sounds of that disaster, see it more clearly, and determine where it is going to happen.

I have jumped from one side to another thus far concerning how I feel that ESP works as far as I, personally, am concerned. I might stop at this moment and say that perhaps like a swallow, that dips and floats on the breeze, so do the impressions come and go. Vivid and clear, or perhaps vague and almost nonexistent. But there is a way that we really must prepare ourselves—all of us who receive psychic impressions—and in that preparation we will find greater strength and energy flowing with those impressions. First of all, sit in a quiet place. Relax. Forget about the aches and pains of your body. Close your eyes and roll them upward to concentrate on the point between the eyes and just above them to the third eye, which is the window of the soul—an extension of the soul, which has an opening that can view the entire universe. Now, listen to the song of that bird! Isn't it beautiful? Do you hear the lapping of the waves as they wash in to shore? And as they go out, do you feel relieved of some thoughts—not of energy—but of thoughts of burdens? Place your problem there before you, visualize yourself as someone else, and look upon that problem, read it over, study it for a few moments; then turn from it and relax and listen to the whisperings of your soul. Please remember that there may be sounds within you since man communicates through sound and through sight, through hearing, speaking, seeing, reading, touching, sensing. No matter how the information or knowledge of the future or of the solution of problems appears in symbolic form, it *must* turn into sound or energy or picture, so that the human brain and mind can discern it and perceive what it really means. This is why I, as a psychic, say that I hear a voice. A thought may turn into a sound for me, even into a name or a place or a whole series of pictures that go along with the sounds. This does not mean that my thinking is distorted or that there is anything physiologically wrong with my brain. It means that I am sensitive to the electrical vibrations of the universe. I believe that this is why some people, when they sit under trees, say that they hear the whisperings of the leaves and that they can ascertain conversations that the trees have with one another. This may seem strange to some and I know their thoughts and the looks they may give one. Yet when life flows out of physical bodies and they deteriorate, do they not go into the soil, and do they not then become a part of living plants? Is there not energy involved in that? So what is so strange about a man who feels that he can hear the sounds of nature and convert them into words, or convert the sounds into sounds that he can understand?

It is a natural process, but it has not been looked upon in this way before. I have always known—even as a tiny child—that man could understand the language of anything in this universe if he really wanted to be that sensitive an instrument, because no matter what language is spoken, or where, or by whom or what, it would come to man in symbols that he could perceive through his five senses. He can also perceive it with other senses, beyond the five, but then he must translate it so that it may be understood through some manifestation of the five senses.

When we speak of ESP some people feel that it is limited to just one extra sense. However, another area of ESP is clairsentience, which may be described to you in this way: Clairsentience is the sensing of a situation so that this sensing is a part of the natural intuitive ability. When I sense or "just know" that something is going to happen to a particular person, I have to tune into it and get the proper feeling. It may be that there will be a feeling of joy because some unusual and joyous situation is going to come about; or, it may be that some sad thing is going to happen to a particular person, and then I sense sadness. Even though some emotion—physical emotion, that is—is involved, as I've explained, I must still say that this phenomenon is a part of the psychic world.

On clairaudience, which is the sense of hearing with the psychic sense, some feeling also comes. In other words, if I tell a person a particular name, like Robert, they may get great joy from this and say, "that's my husband's name." The name may have come floating through the air toward me written out, or I may hear it within me. At the same time that I see it floating through the air, though, it makes a sound within me so that I know that it is the name Robert, and so clairaudience, which is hearing, is involved.

It is very distressing to me that so many people seem to try to create such great mysteries about natural abilities. All they need to do is to have experiences in this way to understand fully how extrasensory perception works. To me, clairvoyance and clairaudience, clairsentience, psychometry, and all the others are a phase of the extra senses, and not apart or different from ESP. Some researchers say that ESP involves only the sixth sense and telepathy, which is untrue as far as I am concerned. I feel that extrasensory perception is used somewhat like a household word to cover the whole field of parapsychology. I have only mentioned a few of the phases of this field; there are numerous others, such as thought-photography and psychokinetics.

Often people ask me if am I religious. I tell them that I feel that I am a spiritual person, but that I am not particularly religious. To be religious means to go to church or to participate in services all the time whether you get anything out of it or not. I feel that spiritual experiences are far more important than religious experiences. More than that, I do not put too much stock in the religious teachings of the day since I have studied Bible history myself and know of the numerous mistakes and errors that have been made by many clergymen in their interpretation of the scriptures. It is really difficult for me to understand the tendency of most ministers to place such great emphasis upon what I would call the social gospel. In other words, they slant their work outward, into social activities, instead of really working with the spiritual nature of man, as they should. The social problems will eternally need solutions, and ministers who are using all of their efforts in that way are really not spiritually oriented. They feel that it is God's work that they are doing, and yet they are neglecting the church and the organizations within the church in not teaching the word of God, and in going out and trying to create revolutions in the social-action side of life.

There is indeed a horrible spiritual poverty in all this and the situation really needs help from those who are learned in spiritual affairs. Therefore, I consider the coming years a challenge to man to become aware of his own spirituality and I urge him to read many books in the field of parapsychology so that he may understand his spiritual self better. That is the way that he will learn about it; not in the things taught in the churches. I am not against the churches but I do want to indicate how lacking they are.

For example, I go to church on Sunday morning and sit there listening to the sermon presented by the minister. All during this time I am thinking about the everyday things of life that need taking care of; he has not captured my mind, much less my heart. More than that, he is expounding upon old ideas which are totally obsolete. Then he goes on to suggest a modern book to read. However, the book that he suggests does fit into this field because it involves prayer. "What do you know?" I asked myself. "He really is interested in ESP." As I watched him it seemed to me that his eyes said "I need something myself—I need more spiritual food myself but where am I going to get it?" I felt like walking up to him afterward and telling him to become more involved in parapsychology; he would then be more capable of bringing a deep spiritual message to his people. Perhaps he could even practice a few moments of meditation and quiet at the beginning of his sermon to get people in the proper mood and not preach so much of hell-fire and damnation that only takes them away from the thought of loving God and puts fear in them instead. God is to be loved, not to be hated and feared. He taught love and that is what His whole world is based upon.

Therefore, if we love and if we allow that energy which we call love to work, then it will bring into play those extra senses that we are all capable of using and through them greater happiness will be brought into our lives.

Much of the unnecessary confusion in spiritual seeking can absolutely be clarified through very simple principles such as the fact that man is a total universe, and that within him is all that he needs; once he seeks within—truly seeks within—he will be attracted to that beautiful spiritual self and will find that he has strength for every occasion, that he has healing within him for any situation, and that he has a positive attitude that he can bring out to make life much happier on both the physical and mental plane.

Man is a living soul. He is a nonmaterialistic creature and truly a spiritual being, but he has focused his attention more upon the physical part of himself, which is minute, rather than on the greater part, which is spiritual. Once he totally realizes this, then he will turn to the spiritual things and be wholly happy and at peace within himself. The only way that he will ever be able to do this is through the use of those extra senses which also involve prayer.

The fascinating field of ESP certainly cannot set for itself any particular goals. The only goal should be one of exploration and demonstration of psychic phenomena, using the most consistent efforts to bring about the highest degree of accuracy. However, trying to analyze how ESP works or explain it is like trying to explain black holes in the clouds! Is there a tremendous gravitational force in those black holes? Certainly there is a fantastic energy that will one day be explained, and so it is with extrasensory perception. The energy is so powerful that the more we learn about it the more we can create exactitude in our impressions; in other words, the clearer will be the picture or the images that flow before the mind, or the feelings and sensations that are involved in that which exists beyond the world of consciousness.

There have been many theories, of course, as to how ESP works, or whether it exists, or, as a matter of fact, whether it is just a theory. However, I can testify that it is a fact. There has also been much controversy over whether ESP is limited in distance, i.e., in time or space. Again I feel that it is unlimited, that there is no such thing as restriction of any nature in ESP. True, many people make predictions for just one week or even one day ahead, but most of the greats have made predictions years ahead, and they have proved to be extremely accurate, even in an uncanny way.

The source of ESP has also been greatly discussed. There are people who say that they believe they are in communication with God's Spirit and others who feel that it is a happening between two people or between a situation and a person. Obviously, there is electromagnetic energy that is involved regardless of how the person may feel about it. I believe that the religious beliefs of the person have to do with what he feels or thinks or believes about how ESP works. It seems to me that much work should be done with primitive peoples and, since these cultures are diminishing, there is, of course, an urgency in doing this. I feel, truthfully, that those who really practice ESP are poor families or people who have lived very close-to-the-earth existences. I may get a little bit of an argument on this because there are people who are very wealthy who claim to be using ESP, but in fact are using astrology almost totally. This does not mean that they do not have some psychic ability but it appears to me that some of those who make predictions and who indicate that they have fantastic visions seem to be using astrology and if this were investigated it would be found to be so.

In past decades there were many amateurs who called themselves researchers in the field of psychic phenomena. Of course, they had plenty of time to check anyone who indicated that he had psychic abilities of any depth. So they spent Sunday afternoons or weekday evenings checking out such people in many different areas. Today, I feel that there is a great need for the true scientific researcher, one who can use his knowledge of instruments in checking any person who indicates that he has psychic abilities, and to eliminate those who seem to be one-time-hit people who are cluttering up the field of ESP. I know one person who claims to be a psychic-researcher even though he is participating in very deep psychiatric therapy each week. This to me is an abomination! A person can be classified as mentally ill and yet travel under the guise of checking out psychics. Interestingly enough, some have been able to convince certain people that they can do this, but they have no records to prove it. If psychics had to rely upon such individuals to test them, what a mess the whole situation would be! It is too bad that we do not have an organization that would check out people who call themselves researchers, and eliminate them by the dozens! It is my own feeling that psychics themselves are the ones who should be involved in research in this field. After all, I, as a psychic, know more about how ESP works with me, the feelings that come, the sensations I have, the ways in which I feel images, than any person who may call himself a psychologist or a psychiatrist doing research in the field. Of course, the help of such people can be invaluable and they certainly should be members of research teams.

As a matter of fact, it is admirable that they *are* interested. There should also be lay people involved with a knowledge of the field, who do not claim to have any active abilities working with psychics. In this way a well-rounded testing method can be achieved. It is true that a psychic may not be able to produce at times, particularly when a person comes up and says "Can you tell me what is on my mind?" To me this is the lowest type of question, and I consider such a person almost an idiot—and that goes for those who call themselves members of the higher-learning fields who do not believe that ESP exists.

For an example of this kind of person, there was a man who claims that he is a teacher and parapsychologist who has made very drastic and untrue statements about ESP not being a fact, and also about some of my own predictions which were published before the events happened. He actually stated in several instances over TV and radio that I never predicted the great snow storms that hit Chicago, when, in fact, the exact dates had been published on January 8 and 11 in the newspapers that carry my columns. The storms began on January 26, etc., exact dates that had been predicted! This same individual was in the audience where I was speaking one evening. He did not say a word then; did not have the courage to ask me a question, but when I passed him on leaving the building, his face was contorted into one of violence. He reacted as though he would like to kill me, and I just smiled and passed on by. I immediately got the Psychic impression that I, as a woman, was a threat to him, and therefore he would continue to harass me and to make untrue statements and half truths about me and my work. He hopes, with all his heart, to gain more publicity for himself, because now, believe it or not, he is announcing, both verbally and in writing, that he is doing Psychic research! My readers, beware of such a wolf in sheep's clothing! There are many such people parading as researchers, without the faintest knowledge of what ESP is all about, and can certainly do no good in research, due to their narrow-minded, preconceived notions about it, and due to their own mixed up world of insecurities.

Another gentleman called me, indicating that he was a great psychic researcher. When I asked him what his background was he told me that it was none of my business. Actually, he had never become involved in the field of psychic research before, but had had the honor of meeting one of the outstanding mediums of our day and by meeting that person and having a few conversations with him became a "great researcher."

This same man had been so cunning as to work his way into a rather prestigious position with a local organization connected with research in psychic phenomena. Those who entertained his presence and gave him freedom to work and who actually put him in a position of authority were fooled only because he mentioned the name of a very prominent medium. This person, when checked out, had not had any experience in the field of ESP nor had he held the position claimed for him. He was not able to speak in a clear concise way, nor did he know any way of going about doing research; then he became a leech upon the thoughts and ideas of others and suddenly started a group making great claims of his own abilities. This sort of thing often happens when people are caught up with names rather than with abilities.

It will be interesting to see what happens concerning all this. So many complaints have come to me, especially about this particular individual that I have urged those making the complaints to contact the officers and directors of the organization in which he is involved. I myself stand aside from all this and wish that everyone could have a chance to try out his own psychic abilities. That is exactly why I have classes and have had them for many years.

I mention these things because it is extremely important, in the field of psychic research, that we have individuals of very high caliber: those who have a well-rounded knowledge of the field, and who are able and capable of working hour after hour in experimenting with various areas of the psychic. This should be so regardless of religious beliefs. I don't wish to get into any religious arguments but I certainly feel that the tremendous religious wars are far more bitter, and have been far more bitter, than any other kinds of war. Perhaps, in the future, we will see a very bitter war in the field of parapsychology, with those factions which feel that telepathy and clairvoyance may well be one phase of it on one side, and on the other all those who believe that all the other phases belong in some other area. I believe that psychology itself stemmed from parapsychology and that psychiatry is also very much involved with parapsychology, and that within the next fifty years these two disciplines will be changed so dramatically as to become an actual part of the more basic field of parapsychology. Of course, no man likes to spend thousands of dollars and years of study on a subject and then find someone who, without ever touching a book, and without going beyond the eighth grade, automatically knows more than he does. It is not only revolting to him but it infuriates him; therefore, he fights against such a person, regardless of the wisdom that person may have. I feel that through telepathic means one comes in contact with a transcendental, electromagnetic, atomic power that creates ecstasy when the currents rush through the brain cells! This, then, may even be considered a communication with "God." I make this comment because I feel that man calls God that power which is greater than he is and which overwhelms him. I have some theories along that line that may be shocking, and so I will not put them down here. However, there have been times that I have experienced such extreme ecstasy in my quiet periods of meditation that I feel a tremendous power rushing through me that seems to eliminate all of the fleshly heaviness about me and creates almost total light. I feel that some chemical reaction takes place in the cells of my body creating a substance which is luminous and weightless and yet filled with sensations of delight.

In telling of the three cases above, I have tried to convey the importance of those interested in the whole field of Psychic Phenomena, to beware of such people, who are deliberately being dishonest and treading upon the good reputations of others to gain some importance themselves, without knowledge of the field, and without a belief in it, and without any obvious abilities to prove their awareness, if they have any, of ESP and related Phenomena. Since the apparent acceptance of these abilities, many people—just like the gold rush days—are heading this way—but only for financial gain and for some sort of security. However, there are thousands of honest people also getting into the field, and we, as Psychics and Researchers, should give them our full support. I know that great strides will be made proving telepathic communication as a fact and that the fantastic research, now beginning, of the brain—and mind—will prove that man is capable of abilities beyond the five senses. Abilities that once were shunned and pushed aside—abilities that now will bloom as roses in the desert of man's greater search to know himself!

One of my goals in using ESP is to solve many of the problems that man experiences in his life on this planet. Also, I feel that goals set in understanding medical diagnosis and in helping in that area can be greatly beneficial not only to medical doctors, but to patients as well. It is also my goal to help in understanding the economic changes and the religious changes in the world today. Some of the prophecies which I have made and which have not yet been published indicate a ten-step plan which will bring into sharp focus the oncoming world changes which will affect all men. ESP is the basis of those predictions.

The tests that I put my students through in the classes that I have been holding are very important, and cover all of the various known areas of ESP. The importance of extrasensory perception in today's world and in the world of tomorrow is beyond comprehension at the present moment. One of the goals which I have set for myself, as both a psychic researcher and a psychic, is to gather together some of the most important people in our land in order to form a chain of communication—call it an early-warning system if you will—to be helpful to government in such things as warnings of invasion, of economic disasters, and of natural disasters; and also to give consultations, that can benefit all, so as to determine whether or not given projects will be successful, thus eliminating those which take up so much money and which do not give any benefits to mankind.

The whole world of psychic phenomena has just begun to be explored and the expansion of that exploration will reach to the very farthest corners of the world—even of the universe—with the use of unbelievable instruments that are not even now in material form. So the path that I tread is one of helping to create interest and to give hope and comfort to those who need it, and to always be thoroughly honest in all methods of research and work. I feel that a true psychic must never be wishy-washy nor must he ever say "yes" to someone to please him, but must stick to true feelings, vibrations, images, etc., regardless of what the subject desires.

Finally, in analyzing how I feel ESP works: it is like walking through the fields and meadows of the world and sensing the various fragrances from the various plants that are growing, from the grasses, from the trees, from the flowers, from the foodstuffs that are growing; it is like experiencing the rain and the sun, the hail and the snow, the violent winds and the gentle winds, and also the dirt roads and the paved roads, the untouched forests and the pathways through the forests; it is to hear the gentle streams and to see the waterfalls, to walk along the level land and to climb the hills and the mountains, to experience the blue skies and the dark skies; to feel the ecstasy of the sunrise and the exhilaration of the challenge of every day, and then to experience the beauty of the sunset which seems to be painted by hands unseen, painted in colors which I, as a psychic, can understand because they all have meanings and painted by hands which even though unseen to physical eyes can be seen by psychic sight. And so it is that until we develop an instrument that can actually take photographs of thoughts and project them in vivid colors as they are presented to the psychic, we will never be able to understand fully what actually happens in giving even one impression. I predict that in the future there will be instruments that can pick up the very faintest sounds that have been dormant in this universe since its conception and that in following this theory it will be proven that the electromagnetic currents that flow around us are the batteries on which all man draws to gain insight and to have psychic experiences. It will also be proven that the abilities of man are simply on a little higher level and that the same source is available to all forms of life, those forms receiving impressions on the level of consciousness of their present evolution. It is true, I believe, that the continuity of life is a constant strain through all things—plants, animals, human beings—throughout the universe, and that communication with all life can be had in greater or lesser degree depending upon the abilities of the communicant to tune in to the various levels of life.

3

Methods I Use in Helping Others Become Aware of Their ESP Abilities

It has always been my theory that everything is relative. I believe in the evolution of the soul as a means of eternal survival after physical, bodily death. I also believe in the existence of love. This existence of love, to me, is the unbelievable atomic power from various layers of energy in the universe, from which all of us can, in one form or another, draw on to bring into materialization different types of love, or feelings of love, in our lives.

My purpose in desiring to help others become aware of their extrasensory abilities is to urge each individual that I come in contact with in my class to go through various tests, to read various materials, to engage in various mental and spiritual exercises, and to bring out the very best that is within him. In line with that purpose, I want each of my students to realize that he is a generator of positive creative energy. I want each to realize the Creator as a positive love energy. And I try to help them all to the realization of the existence of Soul as an energy quanta.

Society has always seemed to judge the knowledge a man has as a measure of his worth. I believe that the scholar is the highest rank attainable in our society—not necessarily the scholar with the type of information gained from books, but the scholar who is constantly searching and seeking ways of understanding the universe and the creative energies that he can become attuned to and use and work with during his time on the earth. That is why I give out a list of many books for students to read but also urge them to go beyond it and to read others of their own choice, and to realize that mine are merely guidelines starting them on the pathway to greater enlightenment, and deeper understanding of themselves and their abilities. I want to create in them a sense of harmony as they walk along this path of life. I call the path golden—because the pathway to prayer and meditation throughout life is a golden one.

Do I bring a specific type of religion into the picture? Not any particular type of religion, but we do use the Bible in studying various scriptures relating to the abilities beyond the five senses. This stimulates people to go further and read the Bible and to realize that knowledge of a Creator was indeed given by means of the very ways in which we are working—through prophecy and revelation. After all, man turns to religion as a result of his fear of death. I want to urge man to investigate the known religions, and then to realize that God is within him, and that therefore there should be no fear of death. So the student has homework each week in Bible-reading. Also, he is urged to start a period of daily meditation and reflection upon the soul. He is given picture images to use, and is also given an exercise to create protective energy around his entire aura. It is then up to the student to determine whether or not he wishes to follow through on the daily work.

The first session of the group consists of the students taking a psychological test which I have worked out myself. As soon as the student finishes the two pages of questions, I glance at them quickly because it lets me know instantly the type of person that particular student is, and what his greatest need may be while in the group. Then, instinctively, and using my own ESP, I try to work to bring out what each particular individual needs. During the class, we have a quiet moment of meditation in order to create harmonious energy within the room so that the power to work can spread among all, and so that those who are powerful can give off energy that can help those who are less powerful in understanding and in their class abilities.

The students are then allowed to select a partner with whom they will be working, through telepathic means only, during the week. They are given properly printed forms for home telepathic testing. They are to put down, in the class, whether they are designated as the receiver or the sender on the sheet. Then they put down the date and the time that they agree upon to have the particular test. They are not allowed to contact each other by telephone at all, unless they cannot keep the appointed moment for the telepathic test. They are urged to try something simple at first, such as a fruit or a spice; if they try a fruit, such as a banana, they are told to hold it up during their twenty minutes of meditation, to describe it fully, to smell it, to taste it, to urge the person that they are sending these thoughts to to pick it up, and to realize what they are doing. Then the student ends his twenty minutes of meditation in blessing the receiver and in wishing that person good health and powerful energy for the entire week. As soon as the student finishes his blessing to the receiver, he writes down a total record of what he said during the twenty minutes and that is the report he brings to class. At the same time, the person who has been the receiver and who has sat in meditation for twenty minutes relaxing, and focusing on the sender, writes down the complete record of what he feels he received from the sender. He brings that record to class. During the class, copies are taken from each student, and then each of the receivers is given an opportunity to express what he feels he received. Immediately after each receiver finishes speaking, the sender reads what he sent. Then we determine whether or not the receiver is on the beam of the sender.

It is interesting to note that a person sometimes can pick up other objects in the room or around the sender. It is also interesting to me that sometimes, when a receiver gets nothing and puts "did not receive anything, could not tune in to the sender," that is exactly what happened. The sender failed to operate and was very busy doing something else. That student, then, was *really* on the beam!

Tests of psychometry are also given in the class. When the students first come into the room, and after the quiet moments of meditation and Bible study, a box is passed around and each student drops a personal item in it. Those items are taken from the room immediately and placed in my own private office. Then we proceed with the results of the home telepathy test, and the assignment of the next week's

Bible study, after which we have a short coffee break.

When the students return from their fifteen-minute break, the box is passed around and each student takes an item that is not his own. He is asked to hold it in the center of both hands—holding it in the left hand with the right hand over it and closing his eyes to reflect upon it. He is urged just to tune in to it and to relax totally and try to sense in some way either mental images or feelings about the person or someone in that person's life to whom the article belongs. Then, after a little bit, the article is dropped back in the box or put down on the table beside the student and he writes out ten items that he felt, or ten ideas or feelings that he had while the article was in his hands. It is extremely interesting to me that some students, who have never done this at all, get tremendous picture images or feelings about the person to whom the article belongs. Psychometry is then explained as a means of ferreting out information about people by those who do not know any other way to gain information, beyond using the five senses, other than through psychometry. Also, the students are told that this is an excellent means of working in criminology. I, as well as many of the other great psychics, have done it myself, and I know that it does work. For example, there was a time when two policemen came to my office and brought quite a number of pictures—I believe twenty in all. They asked me to hold each of the photos and to give them any information that I might receive from the photos. As I held each one I indicated to them what the person had done, sometimes the name involved, and actually some of the acts that they had been involved in in a criminal way. They wrote down all of the information and expressed amazement because they knew most of the records of the people whose pictures they had brought. Also, they were absolutely amazed when I pointed out one who had shot a policeman. He was in jail at that time as a suspect. Were they thinking about this? No, because they did not know which photo I had in my hand until after I turned it around to show them. So it really does work, not only with photographs but with personal objects.

Later on in the class, in order to help the students become more aware of their sense of touch we use color-testing methods. In this test, I employ various types of materials of various colors. We blindfold the students and then pass the colors around. As soon as one holds the piece of material for a couple of moments he passes it on to the next person and then writes down what it is he feels he had in his hands. Of course, there are other, more scientifically developed methods of color testing and we will go into those a little later. This is the first simple testing of color for students, and I have to assume that they do not know anything about such testing; this is usually the case.

We also work with thought photography. This is a most interesting area for the students and they thoroughly enjoy it. If they had their way, they would want to do thought photography throughout the entire ten sessions, but they know they cannot because there are other methods that they must follow through on in order to become more sensitive in all ways as far as extrasensory abilities are concerned.

In thought photography, we use sensitive Kodak paper of either a three-inch by five-inch or a two-inch by three-inch size. The students are prepared through meditation and are then given a particular symbol, such as the name of a person, perhaps a prominent one (sometimes the President), and are asked to formulate a mental image of that person. Then they are handed a sheet of the sensitive Kodak paper and are asked to hold it by the very tips and to place it just before their eyes. They are urged not to touch it to their skin because oils from the skin will get onto the sensitive paper and will ruin the thought picture being projected on it. They are given a few seconds to project the mental image they have onto the sensitive Kodak paper and then it is instantly dipped into the developer; when it begins to develop it is instantly taken out and put into the stabilizer. These materials are all easily available in bowls before the students. The photo is then placed right side up on a piece of paper towel to dry. The students can see the images and usually begin to express amazement at some of them. Sometimes a student will get an image that he has not even thought of, such as a cat or a dog or even a horse. This, after much reflection, indicates that this is a deep desire of his heart! But why did this come out when he was supposed to project the image that he had in his mind? It usually is a confirmation that the student was not really aware of the thoughts that he had in his mind, that he did not have good control over his thoughts, and that therefore he needs discipline in controlling them. In such cases, it helps one to go into deeper meditation so as to be able to wash away all the thoughts from the mind that disturb one, and to bring into the mind only those thoughts that one desires. This is a healthy situation: one can create happiness within one's life despite the fact that everything around one may be disappointing.

Once, while testing, I picked up a sheet of the sensitive Kodak paper and held it before my face. At that moment I felt as though I was floating in space and a most ecstatic feeling came over me. I was so amazed that I felt I was going to the highest point of the universe and began to dance out of the room. I put the sensitive Kodak paper into the developer and then into the stabilizer and a lady who was sitting there, to watch that everything was done properly. almost forgot to take it out of the stabilizer. She said "I don't think this one is going to turn out." But she was wrong! She put it on the paper towel to dry, and in a moment began to express total amazement: there before her was the most beautiful face of Jesus! She asked me what I felt and I told her that I had felt tremendous ecstasy, as though I was one with the whole universe, and that is why I had danced around the room.

She and I had worked together for a long time on the telepathy-projection, or thought-photography part of ESP. At about that same time, Ted Serios was much in the news with his ability to project images onto photographic paper in a Polaroid camera. The lady and I had decided that perhaps we could get the answers to some murder cases that needed clearing up by using the thought-photography method. We did get some images on the Kodak paper, but I feel that we didn't go deeply enough into it. One student, however, amazed us by asking how her friend was murdered and who did it; to that question the sensitive Kodak paper gave this picture: a grave with a man's head sticking out of it and a pistol. Also, an initial, as clearly as though it had been written on a blackboard! The woman was amazed and began to cry and said that that was who she thought had murdered her friend. I reassured her by saying, "You asked and you got your answer. Now, see what you can do with that to help clear up the situation concerning your friend." I don't know what she did about it, and have not been in contact with her recently, so don't know whether or not she still has the thought photography. She was a very sensitive black woman, who had very fine ESP abilities.

What is thought photography all about? First of all, it is a means of helping the student control his thought images. The discipline of the mind is extremely important in all of life. It is far better for one to have happy thoughts than to have a feeling of disappointment and what some call "depression." I personally believe that to tell someone he is in a state of "depression" is one of the worst things that can ever be told him, regardless of who tells it to him. It causes him to feel that he is nothing, that he is totally in darkness, and that there is no hope for him ever to get out of it. It is my impression that when changes occur in someone's destiny, such as a sudden job change, even though he may have been fired this relates to his progress; he should feel elated and anticipate a better position. Usually, when something like this happens to a man, and affects him deeply, he is told that he is depressed and he may begin a long series of treatments. No situation, such as a separation of man and wife, or separation from a young man or young woman with whom one is in love, constitutes a need to use that horrible word. If the individuals involved in such break-ups could realize that there are laws of creation above and beyond those that are written in books, and above those that are known by man and practiced by him in religions, they would then begin to take on a different attitude toward their way of life, and would actually grow tremendously both spiritually and in their attitude toward this material world. They would realize that the soul has a particular destiny, known to it before its conception in the physical body, and they would go on from there to realize that progress is being made in their lives. At that point, they could begin to reflect more upon the inner self, and use the energies of the universe that are filled with love and understanding, so as to bring into their lives a marvelous, more deeply understood way of living. This attitude would then prepare them to find a deeper love and to realize that the energies surrounding the people they have separated from are matched with the energies of other people who belong in *their* particular destinies.

As a youngster, I was very much aware of people getting divorces, of the terror they went through, and of the horrible physical problems of arguing and fighting between them. Each would relate how horrible the other person was. It seemed to me that instead of realizing that they had come to a particular point in the pathway of life, and that they needed to turn and go in a different direction, they thought the world had come to an end. Such thoughts had been projected not only by each person, but by others involved in their particular cases. I talked with a couple of them—even when I was extremely young—and explained to them that I felt that someone else, much more to their liking, someone who would bring them greater joy in life, was somewhere just down the road. This seemed to make them a little happier, and then later on, when it had really happened, they came back to say "Thank you for giving me those kind words that helped me to have a sunny outlook on this situation."

The attitude now is totally different concerning divorce—and it is much healthier! No longer is it necessary for a man and wife to hate each other in order to get a divorce—and thank God for it. They can each begin to realize that they are on their way to a new life, and that they need to prepare for it; they can bless each other and wish each other good health and greater peace and deeper realization of the experiences that life has to offer.

In the thought photography project, a student can project onto the sensitive paper the image of the person that perhaps he will meet. It has been done, and I feel quite certain that others in the future can also do it. The student can also have a certain emotional reaction to what is projected onto the paper and this must be explained. After all, when one begins to have a feeling beyond the known feelings it is an extra something. For example, if a student projects an image such as the one we spoke of concerning the young lady and her murdered friend, that emotion was involved with the thought of the death that her friend went through. But it was the death of the physical body, not the death of the soul nor of the mental energies that her friend left in the material universe around us.

These are various aspects of harmony that I indicate to my students in the hope that they can create a deeper sense of the harmony in their own lives.

Another method I use in helping others is to have two people sit across the table from each other, look into each other's eyes for about ten minutes without saying a word, and then write down at least ten things that they have felt or seen about the other. This is one of the most sensitive things that they do! Try it, and you will begin to realize that someone else is looking into the depths of your soul; it is very difficult for you to sit still and to look at the person that long without flinching, or without laughing, or without showing some kind of emotion. However, the students are urged to reflect upon each other's whole life as they look into each other's eyes in order to see if this part of the body gives off any ideas as to vocation, or whether the eyes are a medium through which the students can gain mental images or feelings about each other.

Again, it is extremely interesting to note that the students pick up much about his partner's vocation—without even knowing the job that he holds! The students, it should be said, do not know each other nor know each other's positions or education. They know only each other's names, and they have no contact outside of class.

I have often asked students to stand with their eyes closed, and to place their palms facing in an outward position but held rather close at about the height of the shoulders. This is a protective shield; they then all walk around in the room. This teaches them to be aware of the auras of other people, and they will not—amazingly enough—bump into each other as they walk around the room. The energy flowing from their palms is such that they can all feel one another's energy and not get too close.

Someone may say to me, "Really!" or, "Of what benefit is this exercise?" It is an exercise, first of all, that helps the students become aware of the aura, which is an electromagnetic field that surrounds each human body. The best way to become aware of it is to close your eyes, raise your arms even with and close to your shoulders, and face your palms outward; then walk around a room in the presence of others. You will be amazed at the energy you will feel when you get within a certain distance of another individual. It is not body heat, but it is an energy, like an electric energy, that flows out. That is just one way of helping an individual to become aware of the aura. Another way is to have some students sit down at a table, close their eyes three-quarters of the way, and stare at the tops of the heads of the other students across the room. When they begin to see a tiny fog, or half-moon shape flowing up from a head then they may open their eyes very slowly until they can see how far up and how far out the aura extends around the head. After they do this several times, some of them will be able to see various colors in that mistlike substance around the head. If you look out over a large body of water you will see various colors, from pale pea-green to aqua to deep blue to very brilliant light green. Sometimes, you will see pink or another color whether the sky is pink or not. Rising from the water is a mist and that mist captures the prisms of light—whatever light there is. With the human aura, it is a mistlike substance—electromagnetic—and it reflects the emotions of the individual, creating a rainbow of colors. It is not the life force, but the magnetic field around the individual. The life force, in my opinion, is just about two inches wide, at the very most, and is a very deep heliotrope-bluish purple color. I have seen it for years around the fingers of certain people when we are sitting quietly in the dark, or when we are working in a prayer group to project healing rays toward someone who is ill in the hospital a great distance away.

Since I have designed my own ESP cards using four different symbols which are very significant to all of life, I use these in testing my students rather than using the Zener cards, which were used by Dr. J. B. Rhine of Duke University. The symbols on the cards that I designed are in color because I feel that color is extremely important in teaching. Also, the little book of meditations that goes with these can help the student formulate a daily discipline of meditation as the thoughts are very deep, and the student can reflect upon them to guide him away from the problems facing him that particular day.

We have sheets on which the student indicates the card he thinks is called, and a column for the actual card called. We give the student about five runs at a time of these cards with I, as the teacher, taking one card at a time and holding it face toward me, and then placing it face downward on a table. The students are given just a few seconds to check the list as to what they think the card is. I do this standing in front of the room, far enough away so that it is not possible for the students to see the face of the card, even when it is put face down on a table in front of me. This same procedure is also followed with the teacher in a different room from the room in which the students are. Along with this method, I have devised another one which I feel is very significant for color testing as well as for image testing. I have various large letters of the alphabet, in color, cut out from magazines and from composition papers, and I also have different symbols in color. I stay in my private office, put these up on the wall, then go back into the classroom; I then explain to the students that I am setting up various targets in my private office, and I would like them to tune in to try to determine what these targets are. Then I give them fifteen to twenty minutes to tune in and to write down what they feel they are. They do very well, and if this is done a second or third time, do even better.

One of the most exciting times in the class is when we have the long-distance telepathic test with a target set up by W. G. Roll in North Carolina, or by Brad Steiger in Iowa. Neither Mr. Roll nor Mr. Steiger tell me what the targets are, so that the students cannot pick up, through my mind, what they are. The students are given plenty of time to tune into those areas, and to write down what they feel the targets are. They get excited and sometimes begin to formulate images that pertain to their own lives rather than tuning in to what Mr. Roll or Mr. Steiger are doing.

4

Special Experiences Confirmed in Individual Predictions

◎◎◎◎◎◎◎◎◎◎◎◎◎◎◎◎◎◎◎◎◎◎◎

The following excerpts from some letters in my files confirm, beyond any reasonable doubt, that my predictions for individuals have and do come to pass; that ESP does work and can be utilized in counseling people in business firms, individual problems, job guidance, and career choices, as well as in giving guidance in spiritual growth and in the ways in which each individual can bring out his own ESP abilities.

"I was amused at the words in your little note: had become a leech upon your life. This is true many times in the ministerial curriculum of a Priest, especially if he tries to dedicate his life for the better of humanity. . . . the very latest on the marriage case. The man left the house last Wednesday . . . so your 'diagnosis' seems to be true—and I say that you are working the ways of the Lord and you are a great soul. Gratefully, The Very Rev. TMF."

"I am, amazingly enough, at a career crossroads again for the second time in one year. I have had one job all of my life. Last year I acquired a new position in the same company. At this time, I am being considered for a promotion and I am also considering leaving to go to a new company. Just one year ago I wrote to you and asked three questions. Your letter contained many events which have come to pass during this last year—with amazing accuracy on the timing of these events. Sincerely, N. E."

. . . "some interesting things have happened since my visit with you on the 22nd of December. The name 'Gene' that stood out so clearly in your mind, was a policeman and the boyfriend of a girl that works in the store. I did have a run-in with him a couple of days after I saw you and I had to use my authority to remove him from the employee lounge, because he isn't an employee . . . also, the green car that you saw involved in an accident belongs to my driving instructor. The first accident with it happened three weeks prior to my visit with you but I did not know what the color of the car was at that time. It was a serious accident. The second accident happened while he was on his way to the store to see me—and I took my driver's test yesterday and did pass it with flying colors. M. M. L."

"I appreciated very much your nice letter of reply to my letter to you following your visit to Washington. Soon thereafter, my Chief . . . advised me that he had had a call from personnel saying I was being considered for a position in some field office, presumably a promotion; but he would not give any details. This was quite exciting in view of what you had just told me—to expect such a transfer in March or April. Attorney F. F. F."

"I'm enclosing a clipping from the *Tribune*—in case you missed the item. If I remember correctly, this was one of your predictions some time ago. Regards, Mrs. L. A." (*This prediction involved the shifting around and replacement of top people in the above lady's company—which did come to pass right on time.*)

"I thought you would be interested in knowing the outcome of a few of your predictions. I believe it is March of two years ago when I wrote to you and asked several questions of you—among them being one concerning my husband who I felt was an alcoholic. I asked you if he would ever stop drinking? You advised me that you felt he would within the following two years quit his drinking. Deep in my heart I thought you, so to speak, 'really blew your mind' but no one was more surprised than I was last January 15, when he entered . . . Rehabilitation Hospital in . . . and stayed the entire 30 days which is what is required. He left the hospital and became very active in AA and has been dry ever since. I would have never believed such a change would take place in a man. Now, he spends half of his time trying to get others to stop drinking. Sincerely, E. S. (Mrs. J. S.)"

"In amazement of what happened this past year, I am numbering your predictions from 1–9. (1) You wrote down three dates and said I had a change of life of importance in those years. (2) You told me that within two weeks I would fly to California, see my mother and come home on the train with the boys. (3) I had more troubles from my waist up than my waist down. (4) I would move soon but not out of Illinois, just West of Chicago. (5) I would be in and out of the restaurant business. (6) I would be in and out of many different cars. (7) Before 1970, I would meet someone named Bill. (8) Be married. (9) Be extremely happy for 19 years.

"The years you named are the years I had my

three boys. (2) When you told me I would be in California in two weeks, I said to you that you were mistaken. The next week I was scheduled to go into . . . Hospital and was told by three different doctors that I needed a hysterectomy. (3) You said again, very indignantly, 'I said you have more troubles from your waist up than from your waist down.'

"At that time I had already sent my boys on a plane to be with their grandmother in California. I had done this so I could go into the hospital and not be worried about the boys. When I went to the hospital I was given a battery of tests and it was discovered that I had a duodenal ulcer. Also I was given a D. & C. rather than a hysterectomy. The next day I left the hospital, felt like a million dollars, and took the next plane to California. I stayed one week with my mother. Having already bought round trip plane tickets, I called in for confirmation for my flight home. I received them. Next day we left for the airport, saw the bags get on the plane, and then went to board ourselves. We were told that there were only three seats instead of four. We got a refund and took the train home the next day. (4) We moved a short time later from Chicago to St. Charles, Ill. (West) for business reasons. (5) There was the possibility of restaurant ownership in St. Charles. After one month I gave up the restaurant. A short time later I became manager of another restaurant, which lasted for 8 months. I am now out of the restaurant business. (6) Many different cars—I was a Hertz Rent-A-Car agent. Needless to say, I was in and out of many different cars. (7) Two months ago, I met a man called or named Bill and we have been seeing quite a bit of each other. As for the 8th and 9th predictions—they have yet to be confirmed and I will let you know when and if. Sincerely, E. K."

"A long overdue thank you for answering my letter. I really did appreciate it. My husband and I wanted to see you while you were in Washington, but when I called the Church no one could give me any information and by the time I finally found out just what time you would be appearing, it was too late. Maybe if I'm lucky there will be another time.

"Some of your predictions are still coming true. Last June when I came for a reading you predicted a man very close to my daughter would die, and this person was not ill, that this would be a sudden thing. About a month ago, her 21-year-old brother-in-law was killed in an auto accident. I thought maybe you would be interested in the outcome of your prediction. Sincerely, D. K."

"I wrote to you earlier, in May, concerning my older daughter, and your impressions have proved true, tho there were slight modifications. She did take a trip, and enjoy it a great deal, tho it was not the one she had planned. However, the change in plans was caused by a new job, which you predicted, and now she is about to change to an even better job, which you felt she would do before the end of the year. I did not show her your letter until part of your predictions had materialized, so she was not influenced by your impressions. Thank you for your help. Mrs. E. W. D."

"Since you were kind enough to answer our letter regarding the Holiday Splendor for Central Baptist Children's House, I thought you would like to know how it turned out.

"We prepared for seven hundred and just came out even. As you predicted, the biggest crowd arrived in the dining room between 11:30 and 12. Everything went well and we were able to put $8,000 in the bank the next day! Thank you for your help in guiding our thinking. Most sincerely, Mrs. M. O." (*The above prediction involved an all-day affair, and those who wrote me originally thought that most people—if many showed up—would come late in the afternoon.*)

"Here I am again! Last February you told me that there would be an internal change in my teaching job in September. It has taken place and I absolutely adore it. It has had a most rejuvenating effect upon me. M P."

"I want to express my deepest and most heartfelt appreciation and gratitude for the reading which you gave to my wife, Mari, regarding me on Wednesday evening. It has given me a great deal of encouragement. I must also say that your comments regarding my past were absolutely fantastic in their accuracy. It is as though you have been 'looking over my shoulder' for the past several years! You started out by telling Mari, 'your husband is an alcoholic,' which is certainly true. Then you said, 'tell him not to worry, for his desire to drink will disappear by the end of 1970,' implying that I still have a desire to drink. And I had not told anyone that, after three years of sobriety in AA, I do still have a desire to drink!

"Then you said, 'The period of November, 1966 to April, 1967, was a very traumatic time in your marriage,' which is absolutely correct. It was in November, 1966, that I was put in the Psychiatric Ward of Washington Hospital Center for alcoholism and drug addiction. The period from November, 1966, to April, 1967—the first six months of my sobriety—was surely a traumatic and difficult time for me, and a period in which our marriage did come close to breaking up.

"And you said, 'During the period of June to

August, 1968, your husband began to become discontented with his job.' This is also absolutely correct. It was the assassinations of Martin Luther King and Robert Kennedy and the Poor People's Campaign that played a major role in my gradual and growing awakening to the fact that my work with NASA (even though it was with the Apollo Program) was completely irrelevant.

"Although I had considered writing to Senator . . . before, regarding my present situation, it was your comment about a rewarding and meaningful position which would come to me through a 'specific individual' or 'contact' that encouraged me to do so at this time. Most sincerely, M. A. K."

"It is over a year since I have written to you and I must tell you that your impressions concerning us have all come to pass. We have moved from Chicago to Florida, my husband has given up his business there, and our daughter is happily married. Hope you are in the best of health, and thank you for sharing your wonderful gift with us. Warm regards, A. M. R."

5

Long-Range Predictions

1. More than three years ago I predicted that famine would cut through the United States between 1975 and 1976, and I also indicated that a big baby boom would begin in 1969 and last through the next several years. This is in line with what various scientists are saying, in their urging of birth control to prevent overpopulation.

I predict that some startling news concerning birth control will be released very soon. I predict that our government will begin immediately to step up methods that will change farm programs, so that sufficient foodstuffs can be grown now to offset difficulties that will be coming within two to five years (*3/12/69*)

2. The conflict between China and Russia which I predicted would come about has started in a major way, and it will continue until total friendship between them is lost, and China becomes a major world threat. As I have so often indicated, Russia will not be an ally of the United States until the middle and late 1980's. (*4/2/69*)

3. Good news is that many of the young people who have been involved in demonstrating groups will begin to fall away from these groups, and they will begin to diminish. However, as I have predicted in writing and verbally for the past three years, these groups will not disappear completely until 1981—after a "most unusual president has been elected and promptly assassinated in August, 1981." That will be a rough time for our nation. (*7/2/69*)

4. I predict that the government will begin an intensive campaign against all those who are guilty of polluting the air! It is my impression that research for controlling and eliminating air pollution will be big news. It is my psychic impression that unless this is done, the American people may suffer drastic physical illnesses before 1978. (*9/11/69*)

5. This, too, is a critical time for the Middle East. It is my impression that the countries involved in the war and in warlike attacks upon each other should sit down at a mutual conference table and solve—or try to solve for once and all—the problem of racial misunderstanding. When that is done, great progress can be made in spiritual and industrial growth—both of which are so sorely needed. However, I predict that reason will not be used and that trouble in that area will increase and continue for several years. (*8/14/69*)

6. The pre-Aquarian age is bringing about tremendous changes in leadership and among those in high places—and this will continue. So we will be in for shockers for quite a number of years to come. We simply MUST become more aware of all situations within and without our nation, because actions of every sort, both good and adverse, will be stepped up, and in many instances we are going to be caught unprepared for sorrows and disappointments.

However, the beneficial changes in education, the beginnings of the new economic structure, the breakthroughs in medicine and in the studies and uses of man's mind will bring great happiness to us! This is the beginning of the age when those who "have their lamps trimmed and filled" will be the ones who are ready for the unusual changes, in every area of life, that will continue to come in accelerated ways. We will experience the adverse with the good, and finally will emerge a bright and shining nation, more fully aware of the justice and righteousness of a Divine God than ever before. If ever there will be a valley of experience that will last for many years, it is beginning now. (*9/18/69*)

7. Again, in an effort to create interest in those who CAN do something about the growing crisis in the Middle East, the worst years in that area will be from late in 1978 through the next couple of years; a bright and sunny day in 1991 will bring almost total chaos to that area. Prayers now may be able to give some help in that direction. (*10/15/69*)

8. On the other hand, let's look at the very positive side: better housing facilities for the aged, as predicted; greater computerized facilities for education—and this has just begun; tremendous breakthroughs coming in the medical field concerning cancer prevention, deeper insight into what we call the common cold, numerous breakthroughs in eliminating or preventing viruses that attack the respiratory system, medical help for certain blood ailments; and the greatest of all news: that concerning the working of man's brain and the deeper and unbelievable uses of his "mind."

Those have been my predictions for a long time, and I have indicated that these things would begin the late months of 1969 and go on through the next five to six years! What a fantastic age—always something new and beneficial brought out from that invisible plane of consciousness where metaphysicians believe all the answers are. That's why I, as a psychic and mystic, urge everyone—individually—to develop methods of prayer and meditation that can prove beneficial to personal values in everyday life: all down the line from one's profession to what to wear. (*10/1/69*)

9. Beginning in 1970 and through the next twelve to fifteen years, we will have a true renaissance of inspirational music, deeper understanding of religious beliefs, and better entertainment on all levels. (*11/72/69*)

10. Based upon my own previously published predictions about governments throughout the world beginning to change leaders, these things have happened, and are still happening.

The latest is the action in Japan. Throughout 1970—and for the next fifty years—many governments will fall and new ones rise up from their ashes, but not with the same ideologies. (*12/10/69*)

11. I predict that the Catholic church will experience further distressing revolutions in its or-

ganizational structures, in dogma and in creeds, but so will other, Protestant, churches.

Religious beliefs of all kinds are undergoing revolution, some quietly, but within and by the end of fifty years all will be changed, and man will be a much more loving and compassionate being, because he will be more aware of his great spiritual gifts than ever before. (*12/24/69*)

12. Let me take you on a trip through our area, as I visualize it in 1978. The lakes and streams are running clean and clear again. As we travel the cities merge, downtown areas are clean, with shopping "gardens" so inviting they look like summer resorts. There is a calm over all; it's a bright May 19, 1978. Suddenly the rain comes down and shoppers take to the plastiglass, three-car shopping trains. They phone ahead for the items they want in stores one or two blocks away. The clerks are busy looking up the "all"-credit cards and packaging the items. Money has changed drastically, as have methods of payment. The clerk puts each wrapped package in a special bin marked for that amount.

When the customer arrives he takes his "all"-credit card from the rack, and puts it into a huge monster of a machine; it slides in and his package comes sliding out.

It is now noon and we're hungry. The rain has

stopped so we alight from the see-through plastiglass shopping train and go into the all glass "health center." There we take a look at the various machines filled with vitamins, food concentrates, fruits and fruit drinks, nuts, salt crackers in thin strips, and fresh vegetables packed in cooled containers.

There are no heavy sandwiches, no desserts such as pies, cakes, and puddings, no heavy meats—all are health foods. Most of the customers are slender and vigorous—no overweights, no sallow-skinned people—and most of them healthier than their predecessors ever were.

We follow the crowds to a glass-enclosed swimming pool. What a community project that is, with various health baths, beauty and barber salons and massage rooms—all available to shoppers who want to relax awhile before going back home.

Swimsuits, bathing caps, and bathing shoes are all available in all sizes at this "resort within the city." They are made of soft, paperlike, plastic materials so that they can be sterilized and put back in the coin-operated machine for the next customer. Sterilization takes only three minutes. Incidentally, the bathing shoes are a must—a protection from scratches or bruises in the pool area—but they can be taken off as soon as the bather decides he's had enough of the pool.

Lemonade and fruit juices are served around the pool—all in disposable glasses. The accent is definitely on healthier bodies; and look at the reading materials! Inspirational, positive thoughts slanted to train the mind to be healthier. In these days (1978), it is necessary to work steadily at meditation and positive-thought exercises to keep in tune and above the earthly problems.

As we walk along the upper level of this vast shopping area, we note mothers picking up their young at a centralized nursery; a huge, glass-enclosed affair with soundproof apartments so that some tots may sleep while others enjoy the kiddy pool and space-age playing equipment. All these things will be manufactured so as to give the proper exercise as well as enjoyment to these children.

I predict that you will see these vast shopping and recreation areas within the very heart of our Midwestern metropolis. (*5/8/68*)

13. Cars of the future, as previously indicated, will be much smaller and in different shapes from what they now are. Perhaps they will look like the so-called "flying saucers" are described, except that they will run on highways. I predict that cars will have "atomic" batteries by which they will be operated—not by electricity, but by this particular type of battery.

There will also be double-decker highways spanning the nation. In other words, highways will be built above the already existing highways so that more room will be available for the greater number of vehicles in use.

Along these superhighways will be "serve yourself" gas stations for travelers still using gasoline-driven cars. There will also be "serve yourself" restaurants with food in dehydrated and concentrated forms, mainly containing all the vitamins and minerals needed, with all the bulk removed. *(9/20/67)*

14. It is my impression that we have a powerful and destructive force operating in this country, one bent on waging civil war. I feel that it is so powerful that within less than twenty-five years we will certainly be engaged in a civil war. It will come just before an international situation, and because of it a radical president will be elected. This will result in destructive and embarrassing diplomatic blunders so that the prestige of the United States will be greatly harmed. We may experience a kind of "concentration camp" or see "concentration-camp communities" in various areas of our nation.

This does not mean that these camps will affect all citizens—in fact, they might be a good idea. They would handle certain people who may have destructive ideas about our nation. I do not mean that these people will be handled in a wrong way, but there will be a lack of space, outside the camps, to take care of them properly. I also believe that if certain steps are taken now, some of this can be prevented, and that these forces can be reduced in number so that the chance of concentrated future destruction will be lessened.

It is also my impression that one of these days the capitol of the United States may be located elsewhere than Washington, D.C. This would make me very sad, so I hope that it never happens. In the future, I can see students reading in their history books that this was "the once location of our national capitol." (*9/6/67*)

15. Since I predicted a shorter work week—four days within two years—I have also foreseen a great upsurge in all recreational areas and in sports: swimming, golf, ice skating, hockey, baseball, roller skating, basketball, and bowling. All types of creative work such as handicrafts, will also begin in 1970 and go on for about twenty-five years.

There will, of course, be many new sports areas opened, which will be very profitable and beneficial, healthwise, for our nation.

. . . Right down the middle of State Street—trees and shrubs! How beautiful they look. It is my prediction that this will come about, and that major traffic will be rerouted to other streets.

More underground methods of travel for the city will be realized in 1973.

More open-air dining areas, more evening activities, such as opera and entertainment by amateurs as well as professionals, will be enjoyed in coffeehouses (which will be on the upsurge again), as well as in theaters and restaurants.

McCormick Place, Chicago, will be like a museum of beauty, with open-air dining and many places where amateur entertainers can perform.

I predict the conversion of theaters into daytime schools—this prediction was made quite a number of years ago (five, to be exact), and I feel that it will now come to pass. This applies to theaters all over the nation.

Sightseeing tours will increase throughout the nation. Chamber of commerce memberships will expand.

Individual rain-making systems will be established in Illinois and other areas of the Midwest to help crops grow; very fine machinery will be manufactured to handle wide areas.

A network of plastic pipelines that will spray chemicals into the air to clear smog and fog in a hurry will be developed—particularly at airports. This system will also help to cut down on air pollution in cities.

Illinois will establish a special school to train

future politicians—training above and beyond the political-science courses now available. The new school will be similar to West Point and will have tremendous prestige.

There will be a discovery of chemicals that will create an almost overnight growth in certain plants, such as corn.

Trains and railroads will come again into prominence and will be big business once more; there will be amazingly low fares for sightseeing tours all over America and low-cost transportation systems for freight. (*2/14/68*)

16. With the tide turning more and more to "see-through" things, I predict that more and more household items will be made with materials that can be seen through—completely plastic or glass TV sets, radios, even see-through or mirror picture frames, clocks, etc.

Eventually, houses will be more open to view than ever before. This is the age of inward discovery of all things. (*11/29/67*)

17. Just imagine, in five to ten years we'll be enjoying international TV—a program shown in Africa or Australia or anywhere will be picked up here direct . . . that's a prediction! (*1/17/68*)

18. In future years, computers will probably even control machine tools and intricate ma-

chine-tool production. The knowledge explosion in the next ten years will be so fantastic that the computers will not be able to handle it.

Recent books and articles about our civilization *circa* 2000 have intrigued some of my readers who have asked for some predictions for the distant future.

. . . 1989–1991—Civil war will have started.

. . . 1993–2020—A second change in the legal system will come about and the beginning of the merging of major cities will be seen. I had previously foreseen changes in the judicial system.

. . . 2026–2029—Constitution of the United States changed. It will no longer be as it was originally written. By this I mean that there will be a complete change; this will be very good. During these years some of the most brilliant men in our nation will come to the fore—in politics, medicine, and other sciences.

. . . 2035–2046—A space war with missiles between major nations for territorial rights on other planets will be waged.

. . . 2046—Another tremendous baby boom. New natural metals will be discovered on other planets and in the bowels of the earth. (*1/31/68*)

19. I have previously predicted that cars will begin to appear in the shape of flying saucers—

somewhat round—so that a protective rail around them can easily be used.

Also, cars will begin to appear in polka dots, stripes, and other designs. Colors will be bright and cheerful and with unusual artistic designs on the exterior. It will be much easier for police to catch getaway cars involved in robberies, etc.

Just imagine a policeman giving a description of a car in this way: "A Model S, with pink flowers on a white background, bearing license number 000 00 000, was seen speeding away from the scene of an accident involving a lime-green and blue-striped Model M, license number 000 00 000.

I predict that in the future, license plates will have the same number as the owner's Social Security number—this will make for less numbers, and will also be an easy way to recognize any car involved in crime.

First-aid stations will be established along major highways. There will be repair stations along the highways where a radar-control panel will have a variety of buttons which, when pushed, will do great things for motorists, like sending out electronic waves to pull you in when you find that your car won't run!

Oxygen masks will be a must in cars, and as previously predicted, electronic or atomic batteries that will last for two to three years will be the main power in running cars.

The centrally located repair stations noted

above will also be clearing stations for first aid and other assistance.

Every car will have a means of communication installed so that an intercom call or phone call can be made to a repair station. Ambulances could then be summoned in accident cases, and the first-aid stations will be able to send ambulances out and prepare to give immediate medical aid to those needing it. (*2/28/68*)

20. Several months ago I told friends of my unusual prediction about insurance: I predict that in a very few years we will have what is known as "divorce" insurance, and that it will become almost compulsory when marriage takes place.

It's my psychic impression that it would be a marvelous aid to both parties involved in divorce. (*4/2/69*)

21. Look for some upsets in forthcoming governmental elections in Germany, and for intensified military training of German youth. It is my psychic impression that regardless of reports stating otherwise, a Nazi-like enthusiasm will rise again, and Germans will be on the march in war within twenty-five years. (*9/4/69*)

22. Life and living similar to the 1880's will begin to come back into being. At the same time

that some are creating elegance in big old houses and barns, very modern and sparsely furnished plastic houses will appear.

This is truly the age of "do your own thing" —and that will apply to divorces. There will be a greater number than ever, reaching to top-level people. (*12/24/69*)

23. It is my psychic impression that the growing and heretofore quiet number of armed whites will break into the news early in 1970 and will, as the next two years come on, overshadow the black rioters for awhile. This, in my psychic impressions, indicates a trend toward some kind of a civil war—a prediction published by me several years ago indicating that we were headed in that direction.

This is one of the major problems—really the most important—of our time, and it is my psychic impression that our government will begin to watch ever more closely the actions of dissident groups, because it will be discovered that an agreement between certain of these groups and enemy nations is in effect, and the news will be shocking.

However, ESP indicates to me that this agreement will not be discovered until much destruction has taken place. (*1/14/70*)

24. New methods of teaching will bring joy to many students, and the prediction I made

and published several years ago about schools "going to the community," with students, using small cubicles, enjoying visual and audio-visual instructions, pushing computer-like buttons on machines to indicate their answers, and getting a slip showing their results, will begin to come into being late in 1970 and continue through the next ten years. (*1/14/70*)

25. Oceanography will be an extremely popular profession by 1980.

Hypnosis and autosuggestion, used so much in birth control, will become common practice. And, of course, that atomizer spray I've already predicted for birth control will become a reality!

Baldness will be a thing of the past by 1976, because of scientific breakthroughs in the seeding of hair. Man will be bald only if he desires to be!

Industry will be highly developed and its great progress will be out as news, between 1970–1972.

My previous psychic impression of Red China's admittance to the U.N. will become a reality, and there will be other deals made with China by the United States to bring an end to the Vietnam War.

In the 1970's and 1980's it will be China in the headlines as it was Germany and Hitler in the 1930's—in acts of aggression, unusual atomic weapons, greater air- and ground-transportation methods.

Germany will also be a source of much news, with economic difficulties of a serious nature, in 1972; and Germany will be unified between 1974 and 1978.

Russia will go ahead of the United States in the space program during the 1970's. (*1/21/70*)

26. During the 1970's, news of proposed changes in China's marriage-and-divorce laws will come out. I predict that the first news about this situation will come out this year, possibly during the latter half. That nation will announce unusual air-transportation facilities during the 1970's as well as new-type missiles. I predict that China will launch an amazing and successful space program within the next twenty-one years, toward the very end of that time —so one can say that it will really begin in twenty-one years. (*2/22/70*)

27. Look for some interesting and dramatic news concerning dentistry and the emphasis that will be laid on beautiful smiles—hence there will be more attention paid to teeth. Why not have a method of dissolving those teeth that need to be pulled rather than the painful pulling of them? (Of course, there are very modern methods of "painless" dentistry.)

Maybe the idea of dissolving teeth will come about, without harm to the gums—who's the genius in this type of scientific breakthrough? I've probably picked up, "telepathically," your thoughts and ideas, and am making a prediction based on them. *(3/11/70)*

28. Fantasy will become reality in the age of computers and data processing in 2000 for planet Earth. Some of my predictions concerning this have been published for at least five years. Others have not as yet been published, but have been written down, waiting for the proper time to bring them out.

We'll have double-decker highways (plenty of space between, since the second deck will not be exactly above the first level). Along the highways will be atomic-battery stations, where motorists can put in their "money cards" (similar to our credit cards of today), and get another three-year atomic battery (which will be the sole power that operates their cars).

Of course, a computer will run the battery station. By pushing a particular button, the battery of proper size and shape will come out and be "delivered" right up to the car window, so that the operator will not have to get out. He'll simply take the battery, put it in a slot on the computerboard (no longer the dashboard), and take off.

I predict that cars, shaped like flying saucers

or ovals, will have a rubberized or metal guard-rail encircling them.

Passengers will sit in a circle or semicircle and will not have to do too much about steering the "datacar" once the direction and speed have been set. A "panic" button will automatically go on to warn of an accident a mile or so away, and the "datarized" gears will go into operation, steering the car safely onto an emergency route around the accident.

This will allow the "mobile datahospital" to arrive without delay to give medical aid or perform operations—whatever is necessary—immediately.

The datahospital will be staffed with two doctors, a nurse, and special "datacomputer" equipment for "datarays," "com-operations," etc. The mobile datahospital will have all necessary facilities for delivering babies and performing the most delicate operations.

I predict that beauty salons, almost totally computerized, will be in existence. Ladies will sit in small enclosures, push a button, and get a shampoo. Another button will control slender plastic fingers that will press down on the hair, and set it; then soft breezes from the computer will gently blow it dry and into place.

At the same time, the lady can get a manicure—but it will be different! The computer will do ALL the fingernails at once, gently scrubbing them after removing the old polish.

Then hand-shaped elements will work on each finger individually but simultaneously: a manicure in ten minutes instead of an hour!

There will be computervision. A set will be installed in a computer-like structure, and buttons pushed will bring instant scenes and news from other nations while it is happening. One will not have to wait for film to be flown across the oceans of the world.

Individual computers, installed in all government offices, so that supervisors can see just what employees are doing in any area of the building, and instruct them, will be in use. These will also be used in major companies for the same purposes.

The Chief Executive will, in the year 2000, go inside a comfortable studio built into the computer to engage in his world computer-datavision programs. This will be a safety measure, and there will be bulletproof walls for the studio—which will be elegantly furnished, air conditioned, and free of pollution. We'll be able to see the actions and hear the speeches of world leaders.

Police cars will be called by such names as "datapatrol" and will have "datavision" instrument panels that will bring them a view of what is happening on their beats (several miles in each direction). This will make for greater safety in the cities.

The most exciting computer of all will be the

one that can "pick up" the voices of people who have passed away—even hundreds of years ago! They will pick up all the different languages, then program and interpret the languages spoken!

The powerful "dataseer" (or "dataprophet") will weekly indicate what to expect in terms of accidents—where they will happen and how to avoid some of them—and will also predict the weather—accurately!

I predict that there will be "dataco" Detect-a-Quake instruments placed in areas where earthquakes are expected to happen, and that these instruments will send out alarms twenty-four hours before quakes occur, giving details of how damaging they will be—BUT only after some psychic has predicted the exact date in the first place!

Men will visit "hair-seeding" stations—all under computer-data control—and will once again enjoy having hair.

Ladies, as well as men, will enjoy visiting the "fashiondata" center, where they will select material by pushing buttons; they will push other buttons indicating their various measurements, and in one hour a dress or suit will appear—custom made!

All phones will have small datavision windows so that people can definitely see each other when telephoning.

There will even be computerized baths in

community hospital centers. The patient will be lifted onto a very colorful plastic, ribbed tray the size of a bathtub and slowly moved through a "datacenter" that will put a plastic cap over the face and head, gently bathe, massage, and dry him with soft breezes blown from the computerized bath equipment, then return him to bed!

I predict that there will be computerized baby-sitters with soft, lullaby-like music playing each time the baby awakens; also, soft, hand-like elements will reach out and stroke the child. These machines will be so sensitive that when a child gives out a cry, the computerized sitter will make certain his face is uncovered and that he is in no danger of suffocating.

If the baby rolls too far from the computerized sitter, the hand-like elements will reach out and return the baby to within the protective area. Can anyone break in while a computer is baby-sitting? Indeed not! The moment someone tries to break in without sounding the special code, knock, or bell signal, the computer baby-sitter will immediately flash an alarm to the datapatrol and get immediate response.

I've already predicted that a home-computer datacenter will be common; it will usually be installed in the kitchen.

The lady of the house will push a button and start dinner, set the timer for vacuuming the house, turn the music button to soothe the children, set the telephone-answering element and take off. After hours of swimming, golfing, visiting, or shopping, she will return home to find the house clean, dinner cooked, the children happy, and the phone messages properly recorded. (*4/8/70*)

6

My Own Ideas of Psychic Research—Now and One Hundred Years from Now

It is an awesome thing for anyone to try to project himself into a world where he will know the faults of people—their weaknesses and their illnesses, their misfortunes and their successes. When I, as a psychic, open my spiritual eyes, all of these things about an individual come into focus, regardless of my educational training. I cannot possibly help it if I know more, say, about combining liquids to get a particular chemical than a chemist or another kind of scientist who has studied for years. It just seems that the whole formula is right there! However, scientists are not willing to accept this because they feel I do not deserve to know. They express their sadness at my foolishness in thinking that I know, without even trying to check it out. To me, it is a very narrow-minded person who has decided that what he has learned from someone else's books is the only truth. Of course, human jealousy enters into the picture as well, since how can a man accept something from someone who does not know what he is talking about? To me, this is the beginning of the basis of scientific research. If I, as a psychic, say to a particular chemist, that if you combine this element and this element and you get your answer to that particular problem and it works, why does that chemist not check further and try to determine what else I might do to help him? The situation described really happened and the chemist decided that he would go ahead and take the honor of "his" discovery. He did not tell exactly how he found out that those two things worked together. I do not mind that this person took the honor; all I mind is that he really should have written that it was because of a psychic experience that he found the means—in a most unorthodox way—to solve a chemical problem that he, as a chemist, could not solve.

I would like to cite here one instance which was very annoying to me, and which netted one individual considerable money. One day, in 1964, a very tall, handsome young man appeared at my office. He said to me, "I have a list of stocks here, Mrs. Hughes, and, since you claim to be a psychic, I wonder if you could tell me which of these will go up and which will go down?" I was a bit repelled by his question, because I knew instantly that he was a broker, and that he really wanted this information not only to help himself, but to gain more clients. However, I said to him, "I'll just mark them very hurriedly for you and that will be it." I did and he went away. About six weeks later, he came again and said, "Well, they really have worked. Now, what I would like to do is to continue a research project with you. So, Mrs. Hughes, if you don't mind, I'll come every week and I'll put a list of stocks under your door and you can mark them and then I'll pick them up and we will not need any personal contact." At that point, I said to this very tall, successful-looking, handsome young man, "Sir, I do not do this. You said to me that it would be a research project, and if it is a research project then you will certainly need to contact me personally to determine whether or not this really works. Also, we need to have a third person who will keep a score on it and who can be a witness, and perhaps even two more people to determine whether we are doing it in an accurate way or if there's some better way to do it. A frown came over his face, and he said, "No, I'd rather not become involved in that," and with that he walked away. Obviously, he was only out to find out which stocks were going up and which down so that he could benefit himself financially. It would have been a very interesting research project if it had been done correctly.

I decided, in 1963, to do some research with thought photography and asked a lady who had been involved with the Illinois Society for Psychical Research to join me in my group. M. P. came and we started our project. I had a very nice group of about twenty-five people who were extremely interested in coming on Saturday afternoons to learn spiritual truths and become involved in that particular kind of research. We sat there in my little office on the warm summer afternoons, trying to control our thoughts to project particular images on sensitive Kodak paper. We decided that I would oversee the group, since it was my project, in my office, and the people had come because of my abilities. Mildred would develop the photos and check out each person to see that he was not doing anything he should not be doing, such as switching the paper or bringing his own sensitive Kodak paper, or whatever. We realized that these people were honest and sincere, but this was a scientific project, and so this precaution had to be taken. We got some startling photos on sensitive Kodak paper. These are explained earlier in the book. I repeat myself to indicate one of the scientific projects in which I was involved and which I actually introduced.

I believe that thought photography is a very ripe field for research. I am thoroughly and totally convinced that there must be a way that I, as a psychic, can project the images that float before me. There is a certain energy that holds the images there, and that energy should be able to stay long enough so that the mind—that protective aura around the brain—can somehow reflect them upon film. I want very much to get more involved in this type of research and have already started a little project of my own, very personal and very individual, to try to determine exactly how it can be done. I have decided that I, being able to see the images before me, will sit very quietly for rather long periods of time and, first of all, try to hold an image there until it becomes a reality, and then project or reflect it upon film. I will not strain my energies in any way, because I know that this immediately destroys any abilities that one may have. I hope that by using various lighting effects, such as a soft blue light when I am sitting and reflecting, that I will get certain results. Also, I hope that by using a green light or a red light or even a black light, that I will get other effects. I will only be able to explain the scientific aspects of this work through my knowledge of these things as a clairvoyant and not by reading about them or having taken a course in photography or anything else. As a matter of fact, as far as photography is concerned, the only thing I know about it is that if I put a roll of film in my Instamatic camera, and press the key after getting a certain object in focus, that I can get a picture of it. I don't know the actual process of how this is done other than that the shutter opens, lets light in, and then closes. That is the way—the very same way—that the brain should be able to work: projecting out through the aura of the mind and clinging to a particular image that is before me, until enough light filters in so that it can reflect upon the film! I'm interested to see how this comes out.

Another project that I have been involved in for six years or so is color-touch testing. I am extremely interested in the abilities of people who can, when blindfolded, touch materials and tell what type and color they are, particularly in their abilities with color. I know how it happens to me: the instant I touch something, an electrical current flashes to my brain and the color follows. I think that I also have discovered something that perhaps no one else has. If I am very tired and I touch red, the color comes out black—that is, the signal flashed to my brain comes out black! I feel that this may be due to a change in the blood chemicals and that the electrical current flowing through me somehow is connected with them and thus gives off the wrong color. When I am energetic, vibrant, and filled with energy, then the colors come clear and plain. I also find that if I am in a very reflective mood, a daydreamy state, the colors not only come softer, but they come in a rather dreamy state, and seem then to connect with some situation! It is these states that will produce, in my mind, excellent results that flow over into clairvoyance. This particular means of touching various materials of different colors seems to me an excellent way to train sightless people to know colors. But no one, thus far, has been interested enough to do anything other than teach them Braille and perhaps do educational or entertaining things with records. I feel that a person who cannot hear can *actually* hear through his finger tips if he puts his fingers on a phonograph, for example, while a particular record is being played, or if he holds a tiny radio in his hands, or puts his hands *on* a radio, just the tips of his fingers—particularly the second fingers—on it. This is just a theory at the present time and has not been proved. I would like to see research done in this area so that those who do not have their hearing might actually be able to hear through their finger tips. We should not look upon these unorthodox methods—and they are unorthodox only because we have followed certain ideas and thoughts and not others—as foolhardy. We should try everything at our command in order to learn more and more. I believe that man's mind or his ability to use his brain is limitless.

It is my deep and sincere belief that through the field of parapsychology, using just such projects as the one described above, mankind will benefit. Let me speak of a most interesting project that was conducted in my small chapel. I asked various students who had come to me at different times to participate in this particular project. I told them that I could not explain anything about it to them but only that they were to come at a certain time. I then told five or six of them to come at one time, and five or six others to come at another, a half-hour later. The project was to be conducted by J. S., a noted psychiatrist. He suggested that we put one of the study tables on top of another. We put the second table on top of the other sideways so that it acted as a screen. Over this we put a blanket, and on one side of this a chair; we also put a chair on the other side. This screen was set up in a section of my chapel between two doors so that those coming in one door could not be seen by those coming in the other. We then decided—the doctor and I—that we should separate the group by having about six people go into my private office. Those six were put in the office and each one brought out at a given time. The first was brought out and seated in the chair. Those waiting in the reception area could not see what was going on, and so they were totally ignorant of the project. After the first person was seated in the chair, I went out and asked one of the people in the reception area to take off his shoes and to walk very quietly into the other side of the room and sit down in the empty chair. He did. The psychiatrist was sitting at the end of the table with notebook and pen in hand and began to ask the first person questions. The questions were of the nature of his feelings at the moment, who he thought had walked into the room, man or woman, and so on. He asked the person about twenty or twenty-five questions and noted his reactions, as well as his answers in his notebook. We went through this procedure with twenty-two people, and said that he would like to do it again in the future. We have not as yet done it, because we have not had the time. We also had a watcher in the room, Brad Steiger, who was with us the entire time. He watched the psychiatrist as well as the subject. It was a most interesting experiment because we found out more about the people who had been former students than we had perhaps during all of the classes.

We also found that one of the students was under the care of a psychiatrist and certainly reacted in a way that was violent. She felt rejected because she had not been a part of the research team, and went to great lengths later on to explain to a group of people that it was not a scientific-research project at all, and was not conducted in a scientific way, because she was not involved in it. Because of this experience, I urge anyone who is involved in research projects in the field of ESP to try to screen, by psychological tests, all those who will participate. When this is done, emotionally upset people who disturb the whole group can be eliminated. This is extremely important, since there should be no disruptive actions which can create a most improper and negative atmosphere in which to work. Harmony, peace, and a placid *simpático* situation should be the goal.

Some of the students became a little bit upset at the actions of this person, and others were upset because they did not know what was going on. I truthfully told them that I did not know exactly what the psychiatrist was looking for—but I did not tell them that he *was* a psychiatrist. I felt that this knowledge might upset them as well. All in all, however, the psychiatrist did find one individual with outstanding abilities. He was rather impressed with that particular person because he was always correct as to the sex of the person sitting on the other side of the curtain. Of course, this report has not been given to this person, nor has it been given to everyone in the group, since we want to do further research using some of the same people. However, I can assure you that the emotionally upset individual will not be present.

In any research project, the parapsychologist or the psychic conducting the research knows what he is doing, and will not allow an individual who is emotionally upset to participate because the entire group may be affected by him. This is why I mentioned the above incident—to stress the value of harmony in any research project including ESP. I, personally, have discovered that a very emotionally upset person—one who is under the care of a psychiatrist—can be understood a little better by his reactions in a color-touch test. For example, when an emotionally upset person touches the color red, I have found that he reacts violently by saying, "I think that there is somebody in this room who doesn't like me, and they're projecting very bad feelings toward me and toward the room." I had this happen, and realized what it was. That same person reacted in an entirely different way when he touched the color green. He seemed to be elated and excited and said, "Oh gee, this makes me feel like I'm going on a long trip and that I won't have any financial difficulties." Why did he say, "no financial difficulties"? Actually, he did not know at that particular moment that the color was green—because he was blindfolded—and he had no plans for going on a long trip. The color green, however, does indicate money and stability, and therefore helped that person to become elated and excited and gave him a feeling of well-being.

Wouldn't this type of testing be extremely valuable to psychiatrists in order to determine exactly what their patients need? It seems a little unorthodox, but I do feel that it would be very helpful. It might also be very helpful if they then suggested to a particular patient that he use certain colors in his home and dress for awhile.

I want to go now into a discussion of a color-therapy study group that I had in the late 1950's and early 1960's. It was a most interesting group, for which I had chosen six people. It lasted for a year and when it was over many tears were shed because I did not continue.

In using color therapy as a means of increasing psychic ability, we met in the same room each Sunday evening. I had a particular light that I used at each meeting. At the first meeting, I started off with a blue bulb in the lamp. Then I explained what I felt the color blue meant and how it affected us in our lives. I went on to explain what I felt the color blue could do about various physical problems. It is my impression that color, indeed, can heal! We also went through the ritual of the washing of feet at a given time, and in that very small group, I urged each person present to take a few moments to touch each other person in the room gently, on the shoulders or head, letting the finger tips rest lightly and gently on that person, while keeping the eyes closed and projecting a prayer of positive thought about healing toward that person. I then encouraged them to give their impressions of what happened to them particularly, while they had been involved in this procedure. They soon were amazed at how they really could see images of things concerning the person touched. Also, they seemed to become very sensitized to the fact that certain areas of a person's body needed help. For example, one night one of the members of the group touched her fingers very lightly to the shoulders of the person sitting in the chair. She quickly pulled her hands away and said, "Would you, C., please go to see a doctor?" Mrs. C. replied in a very loving and understanding way, "Yes, I will." Mrs. C. made an appointment with her doctor and during the session the doctor told her that she had every indication of cancer. Why had it not been obvious to the doctor before? It was very obvious to the person whose fingers were resting lightly on Mrs. C.'s shoulders; she wrote it down and showed it to the other members of the group without letting Mrs. C. know what she had written. It was a matter of record. How could she do that? Well, she said when she put her fingers lightly on Mrs. C.'s shoulders that it seemed to her that she was looking at a mass of black within Mrs. C.'s body that seemed to be squirming and moving like an octopus, and that it seemed so alive that it was devouring her body; she became terribly frightened. It is well known that this is the sort of thing that cancer does.

Someone may say, "Well, that's ridiculous. It cannot happen." I would urge you not to say that until you are absolutely certain of what you are saying. Perhaps you have not tried this, and that is the reason you make the remark that you do. Please remember that man's brain is capable of more things than have ever been taught in books, or that have ever yet been discovered. I believe, as a psychic researcher, that we are on the threshold of breakthroughs of such great magnitude that they are going to startle the entire world. These breakthroughs in the field of parapsychology, relating to the medical and the mental-health areas, and to those areas concerning the blind and deaf, as well as others, will startle the world only because they will come from what the world calls unorthodox research. I also feel that these breakthroughs will, in themselves, cause man to seek even more deeply to determine his spiritual self and to relate in a deeper way to a divine intelligence. My prediction on this is that these breakthroughs will begin within the next three years and will continue through the next hundred years!

Another area of present-day research that I have personally experienced, involves my own emotional reactions to psychic impressions, when they come. I have watched myself very carefully, from the very beginning, when I first started counseling individuals by using my psychic abilities. I found that I rather waited for confirmation before going on. To me, as an individual psychic, it is very important that the environment be a harmonious one, and that the person dealt with has an open mind rather than an antagonistic one. I encourage skepticism because I feel that when a person is skeptical, greater truths will be opened up to him. In other words, their skepticism seems a challenge to my psychic abilities. I seem to work very well in such an atmosphere, so long as there is no antagonism. I feel that anyone who is emotionally upset is somewhat antagonistic, because he resents a person knowing things about him. I do not, therefore, really like to work with those who are emotionally upset, despite the fact that there have been psychiatrists who have sent their people to me, when they have reached the point of not knowing what to do for them. Some of these psychiatrists have been amazed that people returned and said that they really felt that I had helped them. However, others were understanding and very interested in the field of parapsychology and rather expected such a report. However, one must deal very carefully with an emotionally upset person, because he is looking for something to keep him going in life, and in order to be totally honest, as I always am in my predictions, I must tread very carefully in giving impressions that come to the emotionally disturbed person. I have always made it a policy never to give any impression that is not really a psychic impression. I do not feel that it is my duty either to bolster or deflate someone's ego for my own benefit—I would never do that! Therefore, I do not allow any emotions to become involved in my predictions. Some psychiatrists say that the psychic, in such cases, becomes a fraud and really does allow his emotions to become involved. Psychiatrists who make such statements have never checked psychics and do not really believe that such abilities are valid anyway; yet they themselves indulge in intuitive hunches, based on their medical knowledge, in diagnosing their patients. They may do otherwise in treating them.

This is not meant to be criticism, in any sense of the word, but to be encouragement to those psychiatrists who really do get flashes of insight, above and beyond their medical knowledge, about their patients. I feel that if they were much more aware of the actions and reactions of patients to their questions, they would find out a lot more. However, based on my own psychiatric examination during my testing at Duke University, I learned a lot. First of all, I found that the psychiatrist allows the patient to talk constantly, and to tell all things about his life; then he bases his diagnosis, to a great extent, on this. I, as a psychic, work in an entirely different way. I tell the person about himself and mention the dates and times in his life on which certain situations happened; I bring him forward and then take him a few steps into future time. This is more revealing, to me, and I certainly feel more honest, because most people are not going to tell exactly how a situation that caused them to be disturbed happened. The psychic, however, can go beyond what they say and see how the situation happened by means that are beyond the five senses but that relate to them very strongly. During my testing, I found that those testing me seemed to be a little uneasy in my presence; one tester said to me, "I bet you know everything that I am thinking." I reassured him that that was not the case and that I was not trying to determine what he was thinking at all, but I was concentrating on the test before me. I knew that he was trying to get a reaction from me—at least I physically sensed it—but he did not upset me at all. He was genuinely interested, and asked me for some personal impressions of himself before my test was over. He did not use these impressions as a basis for grading me, but he was delighted and actually amazed, as he said, at some of the impressions that I gave him.

I feel that the abilities of psychics to go beyond whatever a person is going to say, and beyond whatever way he is going to react, can be extremely valuable in the mental-health area. They can work together with psychiatrists and others who are genuinely interested in healing people. It is not only the change in the chemicals of the body, or the shifting, perhaps, of certain substances in the brain that psychics are aware of, but, I feel, it is more a reaction to the sounds of words, in some cases, than to anything else. That is just one very minor observation—I have many, many more, which I have come to in my many years of counseling. However, I do not wish to go into them here but I do feel that some day they could be included in a book on scientific discovery.

Another area of research in which I am deeply interested at this particular point is that of the reactions of people to quiet periods of meditation during which I read a very inspirational thought, or during those sessions in which we sit quietly in the darkness and I indicate through prayer the specific appointment with a divine intelligence which is at hand for each. It seems that the entire room settles down to a beautiful peace! Those who have been hurried and upset during the day seem to find calm and peace and go away refreshed, feeling that they have, in some way, been helped and healed of their problems. It is my impression that even the minister in the pulpit can heal people through his words. As a mystic, I have known for many years the wonderful results of positive thought and of creating mental images of what we desire to be. Also, along those lines I have discovered—as I am certain many other mystics have—the truth, at least to me, of the idea that there is a powerful energy that we can call into play from the ethers about us, when we say, for example, "I am filled with success in every way!" Immediately after this is repeated by me several times, some marvelous speaking engagements usually come through, or there arise some unusual opportunities for me to use my abilities. I have used such affirmations all of my life and feel, to a very great extent, that that is why I am at this particular level of consciousness today. I feel that the use of affirmations with those who are mentally ill would certainly help them to come to a realization of health. I feel that there is a fine aura of energy about the brain that cannot be disturbed, either beneficially or adversely, by the use of drugs, that only words and sounds of music can help. This is my own theory and I feel that if such therapy were to be put into effect it certainly would prove to be highly beneficial. In line with this, I predict that within the next ten years, psychiatrists will have groups of psychics working with them—the psychics using affirmations and the psychiatrists using medical knowledge—and that as teams, they will make fantastic breakthroughs! I feel that the psychic can get deeper into what the psychiatrist calls the unconscious or subconscious of the person, and that then the psychiatrist can use his medical knowledge for the final capping of successful healing. I also predict that many psychiatrists will begin to use affirmations in the presence of their patients and will, in this way, help them to heal much faster. It is a known fact that when you tell a person that he looks beautiful or that he looks well, he immediately begins to feel beautiful or much better. On the other hand, if you tell a person that he looks terrible, then he begins to feel terrible. This is just a simple example to explain my theory; it is, of course, far more complicated than this.

My very simple definition of man is that he is a mass of flesh with thousands of various types of energies flowing through him. Though this may be repulsive to some people, I can understand man better when I look at him this way. Within this mass of flesh is a body of light that is the soul—the highest and most perfect energy—which is the breath of life and the part that I call God within man. Those flowing energies I mentioned are varied in number and in matter, and it is these that keep flesh looking beautiful. I feel that if we start from that very simple analysis, we can hit upon some magnificent ideas to keep man—the physical body—looking youthful always, and keep those energies at a very high pitch so that they can keep that mass of flesh fresh, and dewy, and youthful, and filled with vigor and energy—able for an extremely long time to operate at very high efficiency. I feel such an electricity around me that it is my impression that this tremendous body of energy is flowing throughout the universe, and that it can be tapped into through various thoughts and emotional reactions and so brought into play in the physical body to energize it, and to create greater beauty and better health. I feel that it can actually create chemical reactions within the body. (However, please remember that I am speaking as a psychic and that these are my theories; they are in no way based upon any medical knowledge because I do not have any medical knowledge.) Further, at the particular times that I have tapped this source I have found that I do not feel hungry, nor do I need to partake of any kind of food to create energy. Could not this theory be expanded and investigated and perhaps used extensively in areas where there are shortages of food? I predict that before a hundred years pass, this kind of idea will be put into effect in many different areas, and found to be highly beneficial to man. I also predict that it will be put into effect by more and more business and professional people who find that their hours extend far beyond the eight of a normal working day.

One hundred years from now, this will have been so perfected that there will be little use for all of the heavy foods that are now taken in by the body. It is my impression—and it is a psychic one—that by that time man will live mostly on the energies that he takes from the ethers around him; he will eat some health foods, and some synthetic foods. What a changed world and what a happier nation of mankind we will be!

I predict that that aspect of the field of parapsychology known as PK, or psychokinesis, will be in use by hundreds of thousands of individuals. It will be a natural means of moving objects to or from them to conserve energy or help others. A hundred years from now, a person who needs an operation will not lie in the same kind of bed that is now used in the institutions known as hospitals. Here is the way I see it:

First of all, the building patients stay in will

be made of a totally see-through type of material, which will reflect and deflect the sun's rays through certain colors of that material for use in healing the body. People with particular diseases will be in an area covered by a certain color and others in an area covered by an entirely different color, or reflecting and deflecting that different color. Also, I feel that the energies flowing around that particular person will be used by him to bring close any liquid that may be flowing through tubes that cannot be reached by his hands. I visualize liquid foods flowing through tubes similar to water tubes, and controlled by valves on the wall near where the patient will be lying. The patient will be lying on a platform that is somewhat rigid, but extremely comfortable; by pushing a button he can be moved to any area of the room—out of the direct light of the sun, or into an area of color healing. Also, I feel that PK will be used to direct a posture chair to the side of the movable bed, or platform, and that the patient can then use the various adjustable buttons on the platform bed to gently put himself into the posture chair, which will be able to change positions because of the energies coming from the body. By this I mean that the electrical energies, which I have previously touched upon, will be so forceful that when a person sits in the posture chair, it will, depending upon his needs and desires, lean backward or forward or move into any other position because of these energies being emitted from his body.

I also feel that the floor will be a radiant color, almost fluorescent, and that it will be warmed by the solar rays coming through the various colors in the ceiling and walls, and that no artificial heat will be used; I feel that it will be cooled in the same way. It is my impression that there will be a system similar to closed-circuit television so that patients will be monitored at all times and any needed medical attention will be rendered that way. Either the doctor will appear on a screen in their room to speak to them, or he will give instructions to them as to which valve to turn to receive a particular medication. If the patient is unable to do these things, a twenty-four-hour, closed-circuit system will be in operation to keep constant watch. It is my impression that when a patient dies, the platform bed on which he lies will be released from its hinges automatically by someone connected with the closed circuit system pushing a button; the platform bed will then be projected from the room, and, by magnetic force, put on a track that will take the body to a centralized room where it will be thoroughly checked with electronic equipment. If death is near, the closed-circuit system will be aware of it, and all the modern electronic equipment and solar equipment and atomic equipment will be used to try to bring back the life force to the body. If this fails, then the previously mentioned procedure will be followed. I predict that there will be no underground burials within one hundred years, that there will be chemical means that are not now being used of disposing of the body. Of course, present means will continue to be used but the new chemical means will be much more desirable and effective.

I visualize the locations of solar-energy, rehabilitation-and-renewal centers as being round (some square) houses of mostly glass, made of various materials, as I've indicated. These will be located in every community because the population will be so great that there will be no time to get people to hospitals that are far away. These will be marvelously clean areas and, of course, the communities at this time—a hundred years from now—will certainly be different than they are today, with entirely different types of living quarters. They will be very light, similar to the buildings in which those who require medical help will be staying. The houses will be far more open; of course, there will be privacy, but this will be effected differently than by using curtain materials or shades. The means to privacy will be in the actual material used in the window-like areas composing the entire wall space as well as roof space. Where bad weather is always in evidence, different types of materials will be used. A different heating system than we know today will be used as well.

I feel that psychics will have a great hand in helping the medical profession to establish such centers, and in helping them to understand how the various energies in the universe can be corralled and harnessed to bring in the healthful elements necessary for those who are ill.

A hundred years from now, those people who are aware of their psychic abilities will not be calling them psychic abilities, but by their true name of "spirit abilities" because they will see very clearly at that time, elements in the universe around them that point to the energies being released by the various personalities who have died. They will realize that this energy gives them their mental images, and their other feelings of what is to be. At this time, I predict that they will actually be able to flash on a screen the images they are receiving, and that this will help people who desire to know what is going to happen in the future, particularly the heads of nations who want to know what will happen in war zones or in other nations, particularly if these are detrimental. The mind of man will be totally recognized as a medium of all knowledge—taking into consideration the fact that the brain is the atomic motor that generates some of the energies, which I now call the mind, around the brain. I want to make this very clear—I do not call the brain the mind, but I have described the mind as an aura of energy that protects the brain. Also, in a hundred years I feel that great scientists will gather together and investigate those people who have psychic abilities by using such techniques as closed-circuit systems that will project their mental images on a screen; also, all of the atomic-energy equipment that will be available will be able to register the depths of their feelings about particular situations, and instruments that will record their predictions will also be available. Such people will be encouraged not only to make predictions but to offer solutions concerning the problems that they are predicting will come about. All of these things will be completely analyzed electronically and atomically, and work will be started immediately after an analysis which will take only a few hours. Of course, in a hundred years, this field's various abilities will have long been accepted everywhere by all organizations—whether medical or religious or any other kind—all will be working together to create a more beautiful world for all mankind. It will not be a Utopia, though, because there will still be men in every nation who have not reincarnated on the same level of consciousness and there will still—forever and always—be various problems in accordance with the particular age in which man is living.

I predict that those people doing research in

the field of parapsychology today will be honored in many ways because of the great breakthroughs that they have helped bring about to help mankind. The same energies are in the universe today and certain people—such as mystics—use them in healing. They allow these energies to be projected through their fingers as they touch other people and unusual healings are effected. At this point, of course, these people are called frauds and everything else although they have not been thoroughly investigated and the truth found out. However, in a hundred years, these same energies will be used electronically and atomically, as well as manually, by certain individuals, and these methods will be totally accepted without question. It is just too bad that not enough research has been done at present to determine scientifically that these so-called unorthodox methods *do* work, regardless of whether they are called working through the power of God, or whatever. These methods do work through the original power of God, because the elements of that power are in the ethers all about us.

This touches upon another chapter in this book where I indicate that I believe that there are various layers of time and energy within this world that have never been discovered, and that whatever happens to the planet Earth in the future insofar as tragic natural disasters go, these layers of time and energy will re-create life and cause it to continue forever. In connection with that, I feel that the bone structure of man in future centuries will be entirely different, very similar to the bone structure of fish, able to be seen through when there is light behind it. I also feel that the element of flesh will be different, that is, the actual cell construction will be different, and man will be a new creature indeed.

Psychic research will reach a tremendously exciting pitch within the next twenty-five to fifty years, so much so that I feel that our government will be so involved in it that it will offer rewards for predictions that are most accurate concerning situations such as earthquakes and weather problems. I feel that predictions will be encouraged and that a centralized group will sort them out, put them into categories, and feed them into data-computer systems, so that they will be constantly before a "watch" group that will see to it that they become known to the public as well as brought to the attention of the proper authorities—particularly those predictions concerning national and international affairs. I also feel that in the near future extrasensory perception, and some of the people who claim to be involved with it, is going to find itself in a little slump. I feel that within the next three to five years research teams will be organized by local authorities, and they will begin to license psychics; only those who are qualified will be able to practice; the quacks and the frauds who are flowing into the field by the hundreds will be weeded out. There are many people who claim that they can make predictions, but it is found that they pick up the predictions of others—actually steal them from the public domain—and use them, bringing them to the public at the right time, even though they have been published by other psychics long before. This will be investigated and discontinued. I feel that this sort of action will be very good for the field of parapsychology as a whole. Also, I predict that government grants for research in the field of parapsychology will begin to be released within the next three to five years. These will begin in a very quiet way and will be allowed only to those who are doing extensive research that will prove to be beneficial in other fields, such as mental health, medicine, criminology, economics, and agriculture—any field that has to do with helping mankind.

7

Prayer and Meditation

◎◎◎◎◎◎◎◎◎◎◎◎◎◎◎◎◎◎◎◎◎◎◎◎◎

What is effective prayer? Does it mean that I have to be in any special physical position? Do I have to mutter or mumble special words or phrases or songs? Do I need to say whatever I'm going to say, aloud? Does prayer *really* change lives—and if so, why hasn't it changed mine? If God—or Spirit—or whatever it is we pray to is really an ALL-KNOWING GOD—then why doesn't He just supply my wants and needs without me asking for vague and undefined things? For example, if I want a car, is it wrong to pray specifically for a car?

These are some of the many questions that always come up concerning prayer. If you feel comfortable down on your knees—well, go ahead. If you'd rather stand with hands raised above your head, that's all right too. And if you prefer to lie down, that is also acceptable—I'm certain—in the eyes of God. Man is a dramatic creature, a believer in ritual, so if you feel that in praying you must have ritual, that's all right. As a matter of fact, some of the rituals such as lighting a candle and praying while it's burning, or feeling that your prayer must endure for as many days as the lighted candle burns, or making a promise not to eat certain things during a specific time—all of these involve ritual in various religions. Ritual can be a very beautiful thing: if you have to sit down and put on some beautiful music, or if you wish to go to a church and kneel there in the quiet and silence of a holy place, that is fine. However, no specific words need be uttered, even though the greatest teacher of all time, Jesus, said to say "The Lord's Prayer." No words at all need be uttered, no songs sung, no beating done upon the breast or the wall, no throwing oneself prostrate upon the floor or bed. As a matter of fact, these things tend to take away from the energy of communion and the effectiveness of prayer.

Prayer—effective and true prayer—is when the soul of man stands in reflected glory of the soul of God! When man becomes "one" with the great power of love that holds our worlds together! When man can speak or sing or breathe his heart's desires and feels that his actions are being accepted by the unseen, yet very deeply felt, presence of power around him—then man is communing with his God! And when man communes with his God, he also listens, so that God may also speak.

No, prayer can never change the immutable laws of the universe; it can never change the mind of God! What communing with the God-power around us—and within us—does, is *propel us into position to receive whatever has been awaiting us since the world began.* Prayer is a mighty step in spiritual growth, for it makes us aware of our destiny; of our daily service in this life; of the peace within that we can have; of the beauty of the universe; of the equality of our fellow man.

When someone says, "I prayed for John when he was upon his deathbed and he was spared, and I feel that I had a part in it," does this mean that God spared John's life because of that prayer? No, I do not believe that it does. I believe that what really happened was this: Martha prayed for John because she either felt the need to, as a Christian, or because she knew him personally as a close relative or friend. When she communed with the God-power around her—and really tuned in—what happened was that Martha was propelled into position to "hear," "feel," and "see" the will of God in John's life, and, in knowing His will, she was reassured.

What about the man in the wilderness who lies dying with wild animals around him and with no other human being near to pray or help? Yet he gets well! Prayer certainly didn't change God's mind about him, did it? He was destined to get well, so he did! Maybe there was some soul somewhere praying for all the people in the universe. Maybe, but his prayer did not change the mind of God. If he felt a sense of relief after praying, then this was his assurance that the God-power was in effect and active!

Remember well, my friends, we always pray as sons or daughters to a father—prayer must always remain this kind of relationship. And when we realize this, it will aid us in really tuning in to the God-power. How do I know when I am tuned in? Oh, you will know beyond any doubt. The ecstasy that fills you up to brimming over; the peace that is deeper than a mountain of velvet; the joy that turns into rivers of tears! You will know!

God-power, as the father image, never forces anything upon His children. Being a wise father, he waits for His children to ask. And in the very way in which they ask—is a means of spiritual growth! Each individual develops spiritually as he does physically—he crawls, then walks, then runs, etc.

Many of us have sat through sermons of, it seems, repeating pages of words that are supposed to be a prayer. They do nothing to the congregation but irritate it—and they do even less than that for the speaker! Many theology students feel that they must pray powerfully worded prayers to impress those at worship. Many ministers who have been in pulpits for years cannot pray. Their words are empty, yet some of them do learn to pray later on in life.

Why should God take notice of me? you ask—am I not being egotistical in assuming that measure of importance? God takes note of "even the sparrow's fall." He notices and feels the motion of the wings of a fly—He is aware of a speck of soot floating in the air, and He is aware of all that His children do; for every action in the universe contacts, at different depths, the God-power around us. We, as His image, are most worthy of all to be noticed! Remember, though, that God is Spirit and mystery—and that the more we delve into this mystery, the more spiritual we become.

Speaking of prayer—true prayer—it is my belief that many ministers are pastors of prestige churches, where a lot of money is taken in, and where they enjoy a grand social life within their church and community. I feel that some of them have pushed the teachings of Jesus out of the door and have let theology, intellectualism, and socialism flow in through the door and windows. Is it any wonder, then, that squabbles go on in the churches, that people are discontented, that going to church has become a duty rather than a deep Christian desire to follow in the steps of the Master?

So when I speak of prayer I would like to talk about steps of prayer to help you learn more about how to pray, as it was taught by Jesus. The steps of prayer that I will mention are those that I have used in my teachings for many, many years. I, as a mystic, look at the church through eyes that know and yet are blinded somewhat by tears—tears of sadness because modern-day churches do not seem to be very much involved with prayer, or healing, or the teaching of the gifts of the Spirit as churches were in ancient times. I rather imagine that there would be few churches today that would become involved with a healing service; as a matter of fact, I do not know a single church that has special prayer services today—I mean the old-fashioned joining together of the entire congregation for several hours of meditation and prayer. They probably would not even want to suggest such a thing because they might feel that they were insulting their elite and socially minded congregation when, in fact, I feel that most congregations today are hungering and thirsting after ways of becoming more aware of the great Spirit of God within them.

I feel that theorizing and obtaining as many degrees as possible, rather than learning through deep abiding prayer and the study of the Scriptures, and the real teachings of Jesus, is taking up more time in the churches than it should. If you tell your feelings about certain scriptures to various ministers, they may nod their heads in assent, while at the same time they are clicking their teeth and "shaking" their hearts at such "simple-mindedness" where the truths of God are concerned. I offer these steps of prayer and meditation.

First of all, I would like to give you my thoughts on communication. What is communication? To me, communication is the process whereby one person makes his thoughts, hopes, desires, plans, and knowledge known to another —the primary means whereby one influences another, whether this other is another individual, or the great energy force that we know as God. Experts in communication understand their listeners, know how to phrase and present their ideas, and are sensitive to the wants and needs of their listeners. Attitudes in communication have a lot to do with it and, of course, we can encourage people to communicate with us simply by listening to them. The listener has to be on the same wave length, so to speak, as the speaker, or communication breaks down. In order to be on that same wave length we must prepare ourselves for it. In other words, if we are listening—whether it be to God or to some individual—we must put aside all thought of what we are interested in and give full attention of not only our mental processes but of our spiritual processes to that particular moment.

Personality is also of great importance in communication because people are different, and a tolerance for human differences encourages more effective communication. One need not be a psychologist to understand people; some of the greatest leaders of all time never heard of psychology. Take into consideration that each individual hears the word "the" in a different way and also uses it differently. People do this with all words and speeches, and therefore one must be attuned, in a general sense, to all people and be aware of their personalities in order to communicate with them.

Skills in communication are extremely important; most people could be at least twice as effective as speakers if they would only take the time to learn proper use of the voice, methods of expressing ideas, and other techniques. If you cannot take a course in speech—and I never did—then learn to sense and feel what the other person wants and how you yourself want to present what you have to say, and then proceed. In other words, if you want to learn to write or speak, then learn this way—*do* it! If you want to learn to write, then write! Positive communication, timing, and all other methods used must be correct. Only the party seeking communication should receive it. This means that if you have a message for an individual, give it only to that individual, and it will be more effective—do not spread thin the energy of your message by giving it to all people.

If you are giving messages the source of your information should be identified. This information will then be supported if questioned. Always be sure to check on the degree to which people understand your communication. This will guide you to more effective use of all communication. Do not be too proud to ask others how clear your communications are; they can give you some good ideas above and beyond those which you know and use.

I believe that prayer precedes *all* communication whether it is communication by letter, telephone call, or face-to-face confrontation. I feel that I, as a person, must always be humble in my heart, and ask that what I say stream forth clearly, and that there be no conflicting thoughts, selfish desires, misunderstandings, or any other foreign elements intruding on my messages, lest they be swept away.

I also ask that love embrace us all, and if I am speaking to one individual, then I ask that that person also be filled with love and understanding so that the lamp of wisdom burns bright within both our hearts during our communication. Also, I ask that compassion, combined with our desires to serve each other as we seek the truth, flow through us.

I, as a mystic, feel that communication has no bounds—that love is the energy-force that causes us to communicate one with another, and that love pervades the entire existence of all people. I feel this is true regardless of whether other people are aware of it or not and regardless also of their religious beliefs. My world is one of feelings and impressions of dreams and thoughts. Remember that today people are seeking the ideal society—how interesting that is to me! Since time eternal, the ideal society has been known as the Kingdom of God, or the Kingdom of Heaven, and those people who are aware of the reality of prayer and of the light that it gives in everyday living in coping with material and physical problems are fortunate indeed to be members of that Kingdom of God.

The man Jesus seemed to be a perfect translation of the will of the Father—God. When men in the old days saw Him they were encouraged to make spiritual experiments in their own lives. Many of them accepted His view of Himself as the Son and of God as His Father. And then as they began to think His thoughts, their inner beings changed into His likeness and as He said. so to them and to us (these words are put in my own faltering way and are not the exact words of the scripture which is found in John, the fourteenth chapter, twelfth through the fifteenth verses):

> I most solemnly do say to you—all of you —that whoever perseveres in his belief in Me as the Son of God can himself do the things that I am at this time doing. Yes, you can even do greater things than I am doing because I am now going to my Father—that is in a little while I will be with Him in spirit. And remember that anything that you ask for as bearers of My name, I will do for you that my Father who is your Father too—but also remember that I am His Son to show you His will—is My way and My reason for being His Spirit in this flesh body. Yes, I repeat it, anything that you ask so long as you take My name upon you meaning that you do the things that I have taught, such as healing, such as believing in the mysteries of the Father unseen and His mighty strength, such as perceiving the thoughts of others and helping them even before they ask and in accepting your own great good at the moment you ask for it—yes, if you really love me, you will keep these commandments and I will do for you whatever you ask.

Some of the steps that I use in prayer—in teaching it to my students—are these: The first is to become completely relaxed in body and in mind and to be so aware of the universe around us that we get into a state of awe and adoration. We might look at the sky when it is clear and see how vast and unbounded it is—what a universe! And then ask Who am I? And what is my relationship to all this vastness, to the orderly part of this universe and to its beauty? What tremendous themes are these for reflection! Give up an evening of social activity and sit quietly outside reflecting upon the sky, the stars, the planets in their courses, the light which is known as the moon. What are these and how did they get where they are? Was there some great energy that is known as God that put each in its place for a specific purpose? How awesome it is—how I adore that energy, that force of good and love which prepared these things for the benefit of man and not man for the benefit of these things!

The next step is prayer and thanksgiving and in this aspect reflective meditation is very important. First of all, therefore, one should sit down with proper background influences such as religious or meditation music, and with a few happy thoughts. Thanksgiving should play a major part in the inner person in helping to feel deeply grateful for all of the blessings of life. This, together with the background influences, will create a mild state of ecstasy. During that period of ecstasy one should really visualize the blessings that one has enjoyed. Think upon a divine intelligence that permeates the universe. Think of that intelligence as personalized in the form of God, and then go on to think of it in an even more personalized way: that of God being a Father—not only to you, personally, but to everyone. Then, in line with that thought, begin to realize that if God, or that energy known as God, is truly Father, then he is the source of all supply. And therefore God, the Father, should really receive the feelings of thanksgiving for satisfying the needs of one's life. Now, if there is something lacking in your life, then it is up to you to recognize what it is, and then visualize it and help to bring it into being. That will happen if you are motivated to go in the right direction to bring it about.

One must come to the realization of God and to practice being in the presence of God by actually visualizing an energy force which is all-consuming—all-consuming in that it eliminates the negative side of life and brings into being the positive side.

We should really look upon the man Jesus as a perfect translation of the will of God, as I have said. When we conceive of this we are spiritually encouraged to undergo unusual spiritual experiences in order to accept this viewpoint and they will help us to change into His likeness and His image as we are supposed to.

Then we will translate the blessings of that great teacher into positive action, which will be highly beneficial in all of life. For example, if one is a doctor, one will begin to visualize different or new ways of doing things, or breakthroughs in research. If one is a musician, one may find some new methods of presenting certain compositions or actually be inspired to create new compositions. When I use the word "new" I use it in the sense that it is new to the particular individual, but not really new, since all is already in the universe.

The next step on the prayer ladder is contrition and confession. In this step, one must first of all take a deep inward look, not only at oneself but at all men. When we do that we realize that man is working through the lowest rather than the highest to learn about life. There have been many definitions of man and most of them do not truly reflect the real character or characteristics of man. Some people have said that man is merely an ape who wastes his life in chattering to himself that he has a kinship with angels or with a higher force. Others, that he is merely a sick insect going for a dizzy ride on an enormous flywheel, this planet Earth.

Of course, we all realize that we are made up of chemicals, and that these chemicals disintegrate; so the idea that man is merely impure carbon and water put together in a complicated fashion to dissolve again into the elements of the earth is true—but not in a spiritual way. Man—the real man—is far more than that. Perhaps man did start as an amoeba in the slime of a primeval mud puddle, but that is beside the point. That is not what man really is. We have to look at man's potential. The potential that is inherent in man is the important thing—and that potential has no limits in any direction.

Those are the thoughts that one should be concerned with during the period of contrition and confession. Confessing one's shortcomings, in other words, admitting them, and then realizing that one can go far beyond the restrictions of life in a mental way if not in any other way, should be the goal.

The next step I call aspiration and commitment; this must follow adoration, thanksgiving, and confession. We must be totally determined to do that which we feel is the law of God, not necessarily as we individually interpret it, but as it is given in the original form as a symbolic message. It is interesting to reflect back upon the historical documents of Jesus' day when the needs of His generation and His fellow countrymen were just the same as ours are today. They were the victims of invasion, subjugation, and exploitation, misery and fear, and so it is today. Therefore we still need the vital energizing word of wisdom that came from Him. There is a way and it is through the mighty power of love; through love we must learn to aspire to the highest of self and then to commit ourselves to that way and stick to it. These are things to reflect upon during the period of aspiration and commitment. Ask yourself: What do you aspire to? What are you committed to? Perhaps a total reorganization of your thought process is in order.

Another step in this prayer ladder is petition and intercession. During this time one should realize that God is a seeking God and that He is far more eager to give than we are to receive. This is man's major problem. When we petition God for certain things, whether they be material or spiritual things, we seem then to sit back and watch for a manifestation of those things, rather than to receive them at that moment. It is the receiving that is so difficult. Man feels that he cannot receive, feels that he is not worthy, or feels some other such nonsense that prevents his prayer from coming to pass. Why, when you put a nickel into the slot of a candy machine and expect a candy bar to fall, don't you give it a second thought? You know that it is going to pop out of the machine. So, when you pray, why give it a second thought? Give it your all—petition your Father for those things that you feel are necessary, and that's it. Accept, right at that moment, what you realize or feel you should have. There is a difference between accepting what you have petitioned for and accepting what you feel you should have—and this points up the problem even more clearly. The moment you pray, say for a new house, then you begin to wonder whether or not you are worthy of it, or whether or not you'll have the money for it. You do that instead of saying a prayer of thanksgiving, fully committing yourself to that, going on to petition for it, and then, after presenting your petition, interceding with a heart full of thanksgiving.

In preparing for prayer, regardless of the steps that one is following, one of the most significant things is to approach it with a childlike simplicity and faith—that is the way that we are told to approach prayer—believing and accepting that which we are asking for. Of course, there is a time for petition and intercession, as well as a time for prayer and thanksgiving. In other words, have no doubt in your mind that what you feel in your heart you truly desire and intercede for, for yourself or in behalf of someone else, will actually materialize.

And now comes another step, communion and fellowship. This is beyond the petition and intercession stage because we use it as a doorway through which we enter into God's plans for our lives. And to the very degree to which we accept, and are wise to God's ways, to that degree will we continue to pray and to accept and to receive.

The one thing that is all important is to believe that the Holy Spirit abides with us always. It is the degree of awareness of this that causes our prayers to be answered, regardless of what step on the prayer ladder we are entering on. We have been doing a tremendous amount of speaking during these prayer periods and now comes the time for communion and fellowship. At this point we need to listen with our whole being so that we may hear the voice of God and not just the echo of our own words. It is extremely important that, after presenting our side, we listen for the answer. Listening requires waiting, and during that period we are also working toward our goals. At the same time, we are being still—meaning that we are not putting ourselves in the way of our prayers, but are going about our daily routine, and allowing those prayers to work.

Communion can be soul to soul, or in the communion cup or the taking of bread and wine, or with quiet thoughts. There should not be sorrow but joy in communion because it leads to the knowledge of eternal life.

The final step in the many steps of prayer is social action. Once we have gone through all of the others we are ready for outward action. How can we, for example, seeing our brothers in need and not helping them, go on to say that we love a God whom we cannot see? After all, a true test of our awareness of the presence of

God in our own life, and of our responsiveness to His will can be found in the quality of our ministry and service to others.

Our prayers may start in the total interest with self, but they should progress to concern for all men, and to the betterment of the conditions of life for all peoples. Spiritual love and justice go hand in hand.

8

Why Me, Lord?

I believe what I have been taught, what I have read, and what I practice. That is my inalienable right, and must never be disturbed or destroyed by anyone else. As a small child, I felt within me the tremendous ecstasy of being one with the entire universe around me. At that time, from the age of four to nine, I felt that I was timeless and eternal, that I was the wind and the rain and the snow, and the blue sky and the trees and the grass. I felt that I was a part of all of them and that I understood them and knew what they felt and how they were going to act, and also their reactions to the sun and the various other elements; and I could see the wind—yes, actually see it as it swept along and touched the leaves of a tree. Of course, someone would say to me "You only saw the result of the wind." That was that particular person's knowledge of it, not mine! I felt, during those early years, that what we were told in Sunday school was God, indeed whispered to me, and I had a beautiful, continuing conversation each day of my life with that God. It seemed to me that I was let in on many secrets of this world, and it was a very beautiful feeling. However, when something tragic was shown to me by that God, the proper emotional feeling also came, as well as wisdom and teaching in the way in which I should comprehend it. Then, from the age of nine to about eleven, I became a preacher to my family. I expounded on the Bible to my younger sisters and brother, and to everyone else who would listen. I taught a regular Sunday-school class *after* Sunday school, the moment I got home! My younger sisters were ardent listeners and I tried to tell them of some of the beautiful things that I saw, for example, in trees. I would say to them, "That tree that you are looking at is a living soul. It acts just like you and I, but it is restricted, in that it has roots that hold it down." Otherwise, I truly felt that it would walk around and react to all of life just as I did. Certainly, it had to eat and therefore it did this through its many roots; I felt that when the rain touched it that it drank through the leaves and body of the tree as well as through the roots. So, when wisdom—which is all around us in layers of energy in this universe—wisdom from great minds of many people hundreds of thousands of years in the past—falls upon us, it is up to us to drink it in in the way in which we are able, and to use it in our living each day.

Why did I and no one else around me feel this way? I know that it was because, as I explained earlier, I physically died to this world, and therefore became more spirit than physical substance. However, in putting things in their proper place in all of life, I know that I must be aware of the physical because it is a reflection of the spiritual or the soul, and that I must be able to put all of these in the proper perspective in order to have a perfect balance. Some people who teach about emotional and mental balance do not even experience it themselves, and do not know what it really is. It is not abnormal for a person to begin to expand his inner sight, or for the psychic sight to be able to touch upon time in the future or past. It is perfectly normal and is the way in which man is meant to grow. It is abnormal if he does *not* do this, if he stands still like that tree, and is not able to go backward or forward in time. Of course, some humans are so constructed that anything beyond what they have read or been taught is frightening to them, and they become immediately defensive: this does not mean that they have all the knowledge in life. It simply means that they are not adaptable and that they do not wish to seek to know more than what, say, Freud has taught them in books. I know that books and all methods of teaching are merely examples to get us going and that there are worlds and worlds and worlds to be explored through mental pursuits, visual pursuits, and emotional pursuits, that man has not yet touched upon.

This is just one theory in many that I have. I feel that one should not totally lock himself in a fleshly body. We are more than that—we are spirit, which is the soul of the Christ-consciousness within us, and we have mind, which is, to many many people, nonexistent. However, I feel that mind is an aura of magnetic field which expands the physical brain, and that this aura reflects the different vibrations and movements of the physical brain, and that in those reflections certain images are made clearer to us, and certain thoughts are made more understandable to us. I know that I, personally, first of all, had to die to all things in life, in order to be more aware of planes of consciousness beyond the five senses. That happened at an extremely early age when I did almost die. My first major awareness has already been written concerning the time when, at a very young age, in living in a very simple farmhouse in Tennessee, I definitely saw from the kitchen floor, in the attic space above me, a small creature that seemed like a fairy. She was lovely and her eyes were beautiful and she did speak in words clear and plain. I was not dreaming nor was I having a hallucination, as was proven later, because exactly what she said to me came to pass. Of course, some person, unskilled in Christian belief and basing his total knowledge on what someone else has written in books—and claiming that that is the only way to know—would say that nothing like that happened. When anyone says that picking up thoughts does not happen, or when he says that a person cannot sense or know things in advance, or that no one can know things that have happened in the past, then he—and he alone—is saying that there is nothing beyond the five senses, that this is a totally material world, and that there is no hope for man to experience what the Good Book, the Bible, has taught us about immortality. That is his belief and let him go his way. However, I do not feel that people should ever be allowed to say that this is the only way, because it is not. It is their way, just as this—this world beyond the five senses, this knowing of things that have happened in the past and which are yet to come—is my way. My total belief in an eternal God and my giving up my physical life and relying on the spiritual life to experience an ever-growing and always greater awareness of an on-going continuity of life is also my way.

I have never felt that I was a chosen or a special individual. I feel only that due to some of the circumstances already mentioned I became more aware of this continuity of life, and of man's ability to know and to travel mentally backward and forward in time in order to understand this world that is visible to us, as well as to understand the millions of worlds that are invisible to us. I will speak of this particular idea a little later on, although I have already expressed it very deeply in my analysis of how ESP happens. Man's physical eyes see physical objects. His physical eyes cannot see invisible objects, but there must be a transformation of spiritual sight—that magnetic field around the soul that expands and extends over the physical sight—for man suddenly to visualize things in what we inadequately call an invisible world. I believe that there are millions of layers of time-energy and activity, stemming from billions of years ago, that will transcend our time and proceed onward billions of years into the future, and that we have not learned to penetrate these layers fully. I believe that as a psychic I have penetrated some of those layers of time and that I have also been able to transform my own thoughts of time in order to put myself in a past situation, live it, and bring it forth in words that man understands. Conversely, I believe that I am able to transcend time in future dimensions and determine—within that realm of energy which has not yet become physical time—what will happen not only to people but to nations. It is as simple to me as watching a ship leave a harbor and make its way toward the ocean, then getting a pair of binoculars and watching it as it disappears on the horizon; knowing, that in the transformation of time in that magnetic-energy field, it will suddenly be just above a submarine, and be blown up. That incident may be ten years in the future, as we measure time, but as it is visible to me through the transcending of layers of energy, it seems to me that it is happening at the present moment. I do not believe that these abilities are supernatural in any way. I believe that these abilities of being able to transcend time both in a forward or backward direction, and the use of various abilities in doing this, are natural to man—to every man—and that in his development of physical abilities, of belief in transcending time, and of his very sensitive awareness to everything, all men will be able to use these abilities within the next twenty-five years to a far greater degree than they now dare to dream.

For example, I believe that the energy that causes me suddenly to reflect upon a friend who may be four thousand miles away, and pick up an image of him and what he is doing at that moment, is nothing unusual. To me it means that that energy is flowing throughout the world, and that I suddenly reflected upon that person because he was projecting thought energy about me into the ether, and my sensitive reactor picked it up, bringing to me floods of colors and lights which caused me to know that it was he thinking about me. Also, the energy that manifests itself as a name, borne on an energy flash, may come to me. That is a very simple thing for me to believe, but scientists, even as great as Einstein was, may not be able to perceive what I am talking about. I take that into consideration when I speak to people about these feelings or when I pick up the thoughts of others. I also know that it is possible to project thoughts that can be picked up by others. If the energy stream carrying these thoughts is powerful enough they can pick them up immediately; on the other hand, thoughts may be delayed for a few minutes, a few hours, a few days, or even, in some instances, several years. I know that if I did not know how a particular building that I wanted to find looked I would never be able to use my visual faculties to find it; that first inner feeling is the guide that leads me to it. I also know, for example, that when I look at the ocean I can see that the water is green in some places, aqua in others, and very definitely blue in still others. Now, there are some people who will say that there is no such thing as an ocean and that it is a figment of the imagination. This is a poor excuse that is used by many who are in the psychology field, but they never go on to explain what imagination is! Of course, I have been so deeply steeped in prayer and methods of meditation from the time I was a very small child up to now, that I do not want to use the energies flowing through me in a negative way. As I view the energies swirling about me I know that when negative thoughts—my own or those of other people—touch those energy fields, they create a thick gray fog rather than clouds on a bright blue day. With the desire to see comes illumination. The aura of the place into which one wishes to tune can become very clear and distinct when one relaxes, gives up one's earthly desires, and allows the spiritual energies to flow in and around and through one's entire being.

So what then is becoming aware? The great presence of the living God is all around—in the outside world—and we are not aware of it, except on rare occasions. The living spirit of God is within us, so that becoming aware means—or should mean—self-discipline in the stillness until we become aware of this vital breath of life, this answer to all problems, this peace within that passeth understanding! Then, and then only, do we become aware of God without!

On a bright, sunny day, we suddenly notice that the leaves are beautiful and that they are dancing gently in the wind; thus we are aware of a part of the beauty and the breath of God. Then we notice a little child and we see in that child's face the image of a divine being—so we are aware of the living God! We walk along a beautiful path and notice that the rocks are of all different colors and shapes and that even the soil seems to be of many different colors, and we wonder at it. We know, of course, that there are chemical reasons for this, but where does all this chemistry come from—is it from one divine being? Or are there many entities that are constantly creating various changes in the atmosphere and that cause various areas to be brilliant with color or dull and gray? It is food for thought, something to reflect upon, something to take our minds away from worry about not having enough money to buy food. It is like looking into the face of God, and being aware that the energy in this universe must indeed come from a divine origin and must therefore be respected since it overwhelms us, envelops us, and creates currents of ecstasy and delight and sorrow and despair.

Recently, while visiting in the lovely state of Hawaii, I walked two miles across a bed of lava to the ocean. What an awesome thing! As far as the eye could see there was nothing but this lava, huge formations of swirls and trenches and craters and little hills of lava, flow upon flow of it that had reached out and spread itself across acres and acres of land, all the way to the ocean. But the most awesome thing of all was after walking those two miles and reaching the shore of the ocean, to see the horrifying black lava pouring out from a tunnel into the ocean with the flames still shooting out brilliant, glaring, almost blinding in the light of the sun and with the gaseous smoke swirling up all around and spewing out sulfuric odors as it buried itself in the waves! As I sat there for a couple of moments, gazing on that awesome scene, I felt that truly, once more, I had come face to face with God. Who was I? What was I doing here? As a matter of fact, why was I ever born? The old thoughts, the old questions—those that seem to nag constantly wherever races of men are to be found—had returned. Man cannot cope with such wonder and awe. His brain has not been conditioned for such and yet these marvelous natural wonders and disasters happen so as to cause man to turn his thoughts back to the divine energy that indeed controls all things. That is my own personal awareness!

As I sat there, taking pictures of this awesome place, and reflecting upon all of life, I was amazed to see people sitting around, staring at it in wonder, some of them smiling, some making comments like, "Gee, isn't this great!" I wonder what they meant by great? Did they, in their shallowness, view it as an entertainment? Or were they too awed by it to do anything but express a very shallow feeling—fearful of what they themselves might think or do in the presence of such tremendous power! Earlier I had walked through one of the tunnels that had been created by the force of lava flowing through the earth toward the sea. It is somewhat like a cavern, dark and dank, created by the lava, which is very thick at points, and very shallow at others. Imagine the force of that hot liquid fire pushing itself through the earth hundreds of feet below the surface and creating a tremendous tunnel that stretches for miles and miles! No burrowing animal can match that! And where the lava takes only a few days, in some instances, to do this, man might take years to build a similar tunnel, with great expenditure of energy and time and money.

Being aware of this helped me to feel even more humble. When we become aware, we can put this mighty energy that is working throughout the universe to work in our everyday lives in other ways. This, then, is the kingdom—the power—that we find when we become aware that such power is available. You do indeed have the energy to move mountains! Mountains are symbolic of the obstacles in life; energy flows through your brain and through the aura of the mind and is filtered out in various directions to bring about success for you—but success only insofar as you produce or allow the energy to flow through you. If you are only at 220 volts, that's all the energy you'll produce. But if you open up and become an unlimited transmitter of energy think of the fantastic power and the greater and deeper awareness of all of life that is yours; think of the unlimited opportunities for you to put that energy into paths to success, not only for you personally, but for everyone who comes within the rays of the aura of energy flowing through you!

How do we become aware?

Let's look at it this way. If you were ill and went to see your doctor and his diagnosis was that you had a fatal heart ailment or cancer and he said to you that you had approximately one year to live—what would you do? It would be a terrible shock to you emotionally, but that shock might not show up until several days later. When you left his office, you might go out and have your best meal in days. You might also decide to purchase some new clothes, and then go to a play or movie. Then, you might slowly go home, sit down, and reflect upon the whole situation. If you smoke, you would have a cigarette, and as you sat there reflecting upon all of life the hot, silent tears would begin to flow. You would be realizing, for the first time, that the sight which had been given you was fading, the energy that caused you to walk and run and laugh and play was slowly leaving your body, the thoughts that were created by your brain were leaving, and that there was nothing left for you. Thoughts of self-destruction might enter your mind, but you knew you couldn't do it because you wanted to enjoy those last days. You wanted to see everything in this world before the year was over. You wanted to look at the trees and see how beautiful they are; you wanted summer to last forever so that you could be out in the sun and enjoy its warmth because where you were headed—in your thoughts—was a cold, dark, dungeon of eternity! What a fallacy those thoughts are—at least as to the place where you might be going. Only approximately 365 days, at the most, to live. What would you do? Then, as you lay in your bed that night your thoughts might turn to God and your first thought would be, "Why, God, did you do this to me?" *Did* God do it to you? Or did you, in your carelessness of taking care of that body which was given to you, do it to yourself? Think about that. You were not aware of what was happening to you, were you?

You didn't know that if you exerted too much energy it would stretch certain areas of your body, causing them to become so relaxed that no energy would be there. You were not aware of the fact that while you were laughing and enjoying, dancing and singing, that you might be overdoing it. You never dreamed of moderation, did you? You never dreamed of sitting down for just half an hour each day to reflect upon all of life and to enjoy the beautiful world about you. All you could think of was enough money to pay the bills, to provide sufficient clothing and food and proper care for your children. You might find, in these moments of reflection, that you had taken only the materialistic route, that you have not used your time and energy for the spiritual side of life. Oh, you say, "I don't believe in a God." Do you *now?* Do you believe that there is some energy in this world that is filled with healing? You certainly hope so at this moment, don't you? Well, you are becoming more aware then of all of life. How sad that you have only a few days left in which to be aware. Think of all the years that have passed, years in which you could have been more aware of everything —just a little time every day to reflect upon the beauty of the trees, the grass, the snow, the sun, flowers, the expressions in people's faces, the laughter, the tears, and the joy of others; aware of the colors in your own house, whether they are healing colors or not; aware of your friends and of their problems and joys. "Let them take care of themselves," you said, but now you find that you need them to take care of you! You want them to be sympathetic to you, to help you live out these last days in joy and delight and happiness. But most of all, your heart cries out for healing! Will it come? And then you might begin to seek those who are more aware than you of the mysteries of life. Perhaps, you might say in your heart, there is someone who can heal me. Indeed, there is! But that very person—or that very energy—is what you have rejected all of your life. You have come face to face with God.

Well—let's use the same reaction to become aware. Work at it each day as though that day were your last! Live for that day and that hour only and put your whole heart and mind into it. Within a year you will have made such tremendous progress that in looking back you will not recognize last year's you. What's the good of giving ten minutes of our time if we are not willing to go one more step and give a half-hour?—not to help what we call God, but to help ourselves to attain spiritual freedom, and to accept what God has already given us—a heritage of sonship in his magnificent kingdom!